WHO WAS?

General Editor of the Series: Jean Leymarie

WHO WAS

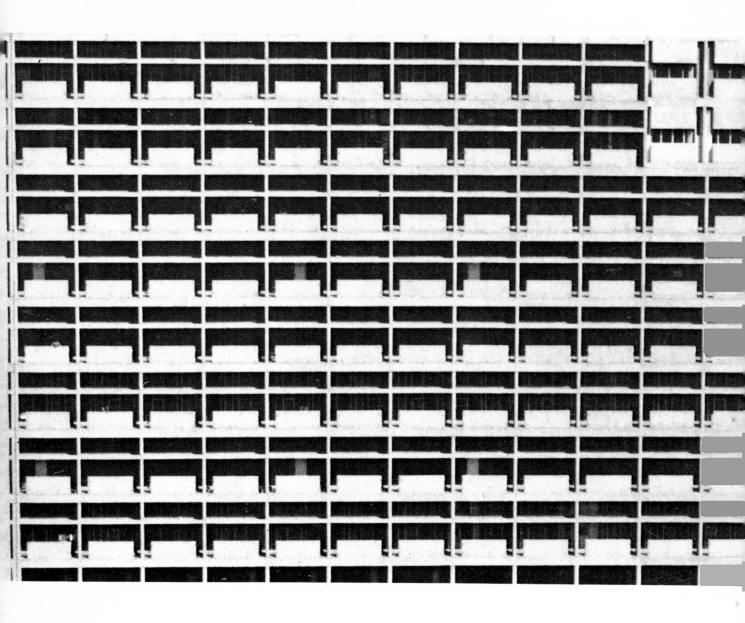

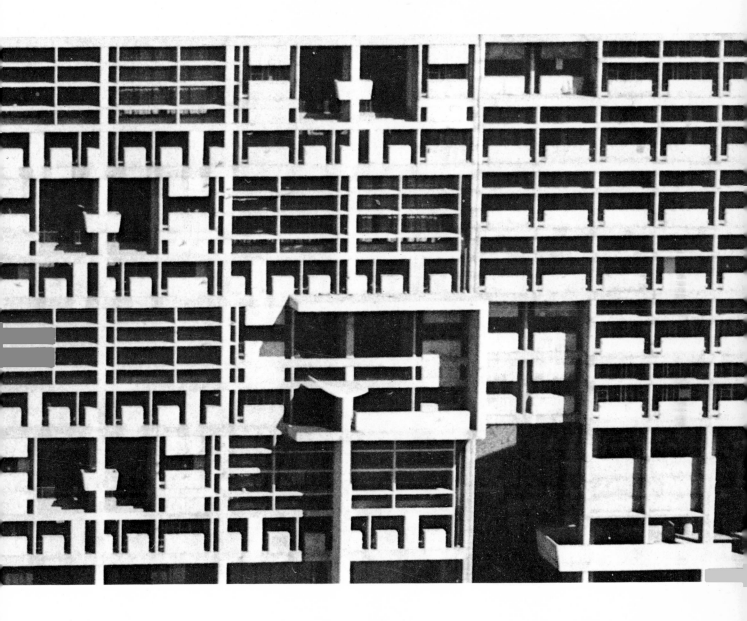

LE CORBUSIER?

TEXT BY MAURICE BESSET

TRANSLATED FROM THE FRENCH BY ROBIN KEMBALL

On the title page:
The Secretariat at Chandigarh (Punjab), 1958. Detail of the West Front.

★

Distributed in the United States by
THE WORLD PUBLISHING COMPANY
2231 West 110th Street, Cleveland, Ohio 44102

★

★

Library of Congress Catalog Card Number: 68-59085

CONTENTS

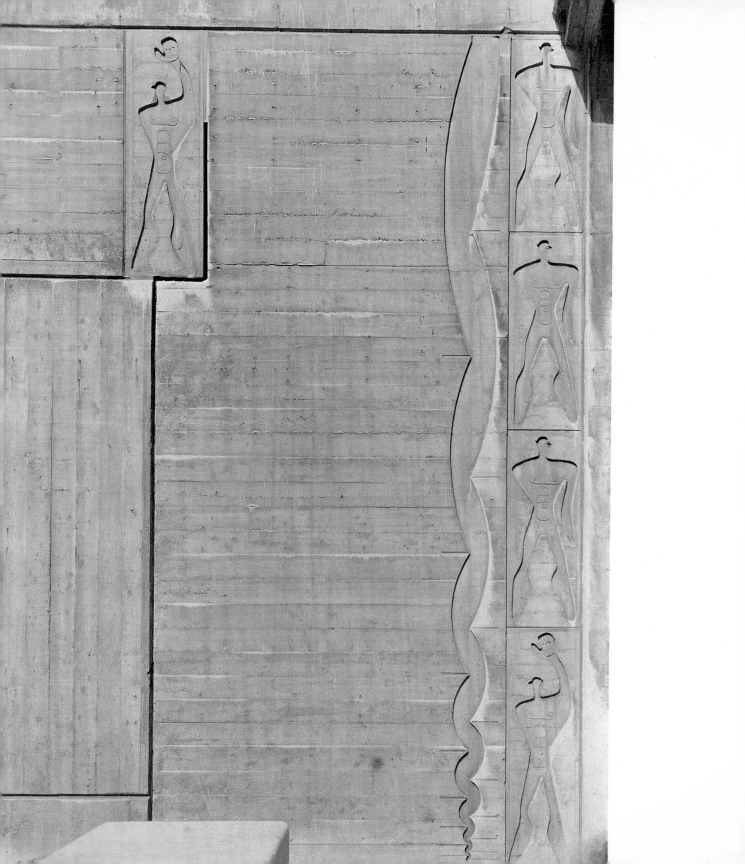

IMPERFECT as our knowledge of Le Corbusier may be, we at once sense that one of the major problems facing us in relation to him concerns the manner in which a man's creative endeavor (whose brutal, shattering novelty no one would seriously think of denying) may derive from a passionately attentive, painstaking study of the world, including contemporary reality, the heritage of tradition, and the laws of nature. From the very considerable sum of knowledge, reading, and, above all, direct—mainly visual—observation that he accumulated, Le Corbusier acquired for himself a fund of culture which not only ranged far wider than he chose to admit, but which was invariably at his beck and call. "*Regarder*" and "*voir*," he liked to say, thereby drawing a meticulous distinction between *looking*, which for him consisted merely in noting, collecting, garnering, assembling, and *seeing*, which signified understanding, apprehending, establishing connections, or, as he also liked to put it, "classifying." Only after this came the process of "inventing" and "creating." If one traces—beginning with each form,

◄ *The Marseilles Apartment Block (Unité d'Habitation), 1945-1952: Relief in concrete by Le Corbusier, based on his Modulor figure.*

each idea, that bears his imprint—the often baffling sequence of these operations, endeavoring in each case to determine the relationship between observation and creative vision, one finds scarcely an idea or a form, however novel and however authentically *his*, that does not have its origins in some concrete observation, some fact recorded, some question posed. As he himself remarked, with some sadness, contemporary man is "someone who knows things, but things he has neither invented nor even verified, and who, in the course of the instruction he has received, has lost that supreme and candid energy of the child who never tires of asking: Why?" The starting point for any intellectual biography of Le Corbusier must surely be sought in that remarkable curiosity which for him represented, not some inert mass of knowledge, passively accepted, but something actively appropriated, a constant, tireless challenge.

Who was Le Corbusier? The traditional methods of historical analysis are hardly applicable to a man who *is* today at least as much as he *was* yesterday. Who, as an architect, is present, in dazzling or diffuse fashion, in almost the whole of today's production and who, in all probability, will still be present in tomorrow's. Who, as a town-planner, is at all times at the center of a discussion bearing on the gravest problems of our environment, our contemporary way of life. The place in history occupied by other pioneers of the twentieth century, in the plastic arts and even in architecture, is today clearly established: in painting, for instance, post-Cubism, post-Surrealism, and even post-Abstraction have gradually gained sufficient distance to enable one to assess the contribution and sense the aspirations of each. By contrast, the stage of post-Corbusierism is not yet with us: the challenge, fierce as it is here and there, has not yet resolved itself into a sufficiently coherent movement to mark the opening of a new phase and, with it, to establish for Le Corbusier a definite place in history.

Le Corbusier is thus a man of our time. But he was also—and he himself never tired of emphasizing the fact—the child of another age, the 1900 generation: a man shaped in the ideological and aesthetic climate of a *belle époque* that is today no more than a legend. And it is in the early twenties, itself a far-off period for most of us today, that we find the great and, for him, decisive adventure of *L'Esprit Nouveau*. If we would place his personality and his life's journey in true perspective, we cannot ignore the very considerable distance now separating us from those events and from their context. Like some great creative figure of the past, spanning several different epochs, Le Corbusier today presents us with a twofold image, and it is the juxtaposition of its two aspects—the one still close at hand and sharply colored by polemical shades, the other far removed and already allocated a place in history—which renders the interpretation of this image so exceptionally difficult.

To this must be added the extreme aversion manifested by the man (albeit so prolix in defending his ideas) to talking of himself, plus the obstinate persistence with which, in an effort to protect himself from the curiosity of investigators, he did all he could to throw them off the scent. Rare indeed are the autobiographical documents accessible today; rarer still, any truly enlightening accounts by those who knew him. In the present deficient state of our knowledge, then, it still seems premature to attempt a synthesis that could truly claim to answer the question contained in the ambitious title of this book. Instead, in the pages that follow, we shall confine ourselves to singling out certain themes whose constant recurrence throughout Le Corbusier's work seems to us to justify certain conclusions (or at any rate to open up certain avenues of approach) concerning, if not the personality of the man whom Le Corbusier did his best to conceal from inquisitive minds, at least the ideas, the methods or, as he himself used to say, the manner of thinking of that impassioned "questioner" and incomparable creative artist that he undoubtedly was.

The Discovery
of the World

TRAVEL NOTEBOOKS

ENCOUNTERS

I became really appalled at the teaching of the schools,
at the set formulas and assumptions of divine right,
and I took it into my head, at that unsettled time,
to appeal to my own judgment.
With my savings, I went on a journey through several countries,
far from the schools, and, earning my living in practical occupations,
I began to open my eyes.

The formative years of Charles-Edouard Jeanneret, the future Le Corbusier, were marked by two contradictory experiences. One was the oppressive narrowness of the small town where he was born and brought up, La Chaux-de-Fonds, in the Swiss Jura; the town had long been wholly devoted to a single activity, watchmaking (at that time more a craft than an industry), but its traditional economic and social structures were beginning to give way under the pressure of growing capital investments. The other was the wide horizons opened up by his early travels, during which he acquired a visual culture of immense scope, while at the same time becoming aware of the brutal impact being made on the world of forms by the industrial revolution then in the making.

At La Chaux-de-Fonds he fought his first battles and suffered his first disappointments, both in connection with that "new section" of the local Art School which in its aims and methods was following the lead of the great movement for reform in art training recently launched in Germany—a movement which at La Chaux-de-Fonds was nipped in the bud by the hostility of the traditionalists. As for his travels, they took him not only to the most active centers of the modern movement at that time (Paris, Munich, Vienna, Berlin), but to the great museums and classic sites, from Chartres to Pompeii, from Florence to Athens, from Istanbul to Rome, and also to some of the last regions in Europe where traditional ways of life still survived. In Paris, in Vienna, in Germany, came the encounters which set his mind and thoughts on their lifelong course. And, most important, all along the way young Jeanneret drew and sketched, thus beginning that task of deciphering the world with his pencil which was to last for sixty years.

It seems worth while, in the opening pages of this book, to reproduce some of these drawings and thus to indicate the formation of this very broad, very open, extraordinarily concrete culture. For it was a culture that owed as much to the traditional world of folklore as it did to the modern cities, as much to the patient visiting of museums as to contacts with the pioneers of a new art; it was a culture which, though rooted in the Latin tradition, was yet deeply marked by the Germanic world. As his prentice years drew to a close, two things had become quite clear to Jeanneret: the whole system of values founded on craftwork, on the manual production of individual objects, was obsolete; a new idiom was in the making, bound up with the new conditions created by mass production, an idiom whose norms remained to be defined. It was the purpose of Purism to define the approach to this problem.

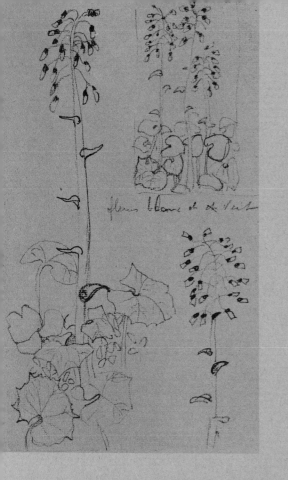

fleurs blanc et de Vert

Invoking the example of the Gothic master masons and sculptors, Viollet-le-Duc had urged architects and decorators to study local plant forms. By the end of the nineteenth century, the study of plant forms, broadened by the observation of organic microstructures, had become a standard part of the rationalist teaching of design; echoes of it are to be found in Frank Lloyd Wright. Then came Art Nouveau, with its one-sided interpretation of floral motifs in terms of the decorative arabesque. Acting on the advice of his early teacher L'Eplattenier, himself an admirer of Grasset, Charles-Edouard Jeanneret set himself, in reaction against the excesses of Art Nouveau, to study the geometric structure of the fir tree, even of the yellow gentian (both typical of the Jura flora), and to deduce from it a decorative system capable of an architectural development. He employed this system in certain constructions of his La Chaux-de-Fonds period.

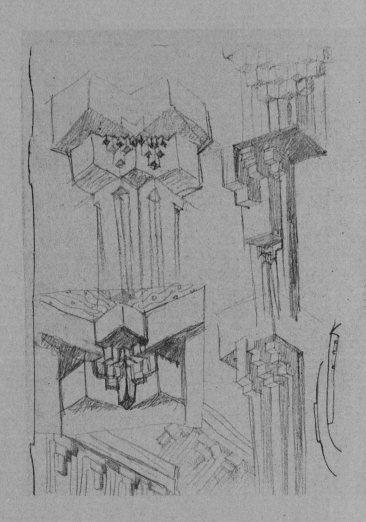

◄ *Above left: Sketch of Flowers, 1913-1914.*
Pencil on brown paper.

◄ *Above right: Sketch of Snow-Covered Fir Tree and*
Fir Branches, 1913-1914. Pencil on Canson paper.

◄ *Below: Flat Decorative Pattern based on the Fir Tree Motif,*
1913-1914. Indian ink on brown paper.

Architectural Decoration based on Geometric Elements, ►
1913-1914. Pencil on grey-brown paper.

◄ *Page 13: Santa Croce in Florence.*
Sketch of the Nave and the Timber Roof Frame.
Pencil on Canson paper heightened with watercolor.

15

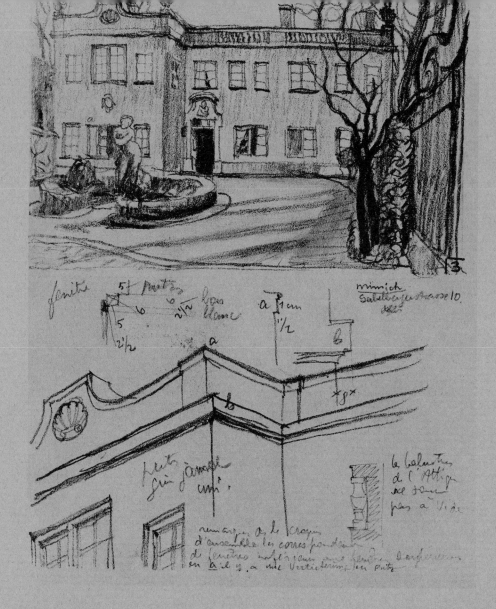

In the presence of a grandiose interior arresting in its utter simplicity, like Santa Croce, or of one happy detail, like a neoclassical attic outlined against the sky, Jeanneret did not use his pencil merely to capture what he later called "effluvia" (by which he meant intimations of an atmospheric or sentimental picturesqueness); he used it always to pose the question which all his life he asked of all the natural or constructed forms he met with: Why? He was equally attentive to the lessons of folk architecture, especially in the Mediterranean lands he visited: over and above all folklore, its science of economy and richness of imagination sent him into raptures, and the sterling example of "morality" that it gave him no doubt counted for quite as much in the formation of his architectural language as did the austere geometry of Cubism. To folk architecture too he owed the "law of whitewash" which he opposed unrelentingly to the "impurity"

"Happy solution of the angle of the wall." 1911. Pencil on paper.

◄ *Gabelsbergerstrasse No. 10 in Munich. Overall View and Detail of the Attic, 1911. Pencil on paper heightened with colors.*

of decorative art: "Whitewash has been connected with the home of men since the birth of mankind: you burn stones, you pound them, you add water, you brush it on, and the walls become the purest white: a white extraordinarily beautiful. If the house is all white, the design of things stands out without any possible transgression: the volume of things is clear-cut: the color of things is categorical. Whitewash is absolute, everything stands out from it or goes down on it absolutely, black on white: it is forthright and straightforward. Set objects against it that are unclean or in bad taste: you see them at once for what they are. It is a kind of X-ray of beauty. It is an Assize Court sitting in permanent judgment. It is the eye of Truth. Whitewash is extremely moral. It is the wealth of the poor man and the rich man, of every man, just as bread, milk and water are the wealth of slave and king alike."

Farm at Muratli in European Turkey, 1911. Pencil on Canson paper.

Folk art, both in handicrafts and in anonymous architecture, has in the course of centuries worked out standards perfectly suited to the needs and measure of man, standards which for that very reason are in complete harmony among themselves and with the natural setting in which they arise. A living organism, born of life, not a rigid or arbitrary system of forms, the standard is defined as much by its flexibility as by its exactitude: this or that "architectural unit" arrived at by the Turkish peasant of the Adrianople region adapts itself to a site in the plain as well as it does to hill country. It was against the background of the mastery achieved by the centuries-long handling of standards that Jeanneret-Le Corbusier saw the great works of architecture: of the Parthenon, for example, he said it was "a product of selection applied to a standard." Thus the great mosques of Istanbul and Brussa transpose to the level of pure creation that science of the relations between exterior space and interior volume which characterizes all Islamic architecture and which is founded essentially on a refined use of breaks in scale. Before he saw Pompeii, these mosques moreover revealed to Jeanneret the infinite possibilities offered by light for the definition of interior spaces, particularly by reflected or diffracted light, whose modulations set volumes vibrating. In these mosques, he was struck too by the rigorous exactness of the relations which, in their external profile, link the hemispherical domes, swollen like bellying sails, with the straightness of the minarets—a straightness upright but by no means dry. Le Corbusier was never to forget the lesson impressed on him by Byzantium and Islam: it was to the arrangement of the windows at the base of the domes of St Sophia that he referred to justify the type of lighting adopted for one of his very last projects, the parish church of Firminy in southeastern France, one of his boldest and most beautiful designs.

Mosque of Suleiman in Istanbul, 1911. Pencil on paper.

At the Campo Santo in Pisa Jeanneret first realized what the "masterly, correct and magnificent play of forms in light" meant on the scale of a monumental composition of an unsurpassed amplitude. There he saw how a single unexpected slanting line, that of the Leaning Tower, could elicit a strong dramatic tension from the most serenely balanced order. It was Pisa he had in mind when, twenty years later, he organized his plan for the Palace of the Soviets around a juxtaposition of strongly contrasting volumes. As for the Parthenon, Jeanneret spent three weeks in 1911 studying and scrutinizing it—three harassed weeks, as he confessed, fraught with perplexity and frustration before he came to see it as the absolute masterpiece of architecture, a "pure creation of the mind." From this conviction he never

Campo Santo in Pisa, 1911. Pencil on Canson paper.

The Acropolis in Athens. Drawing (original lost).

deviated. The Parthenon showed him how an edifice can control and give order to a whole landscape, and how the laws of harmony and optical adjustments can operate to magnify form. A moral lesson was brought home to him by the inexorably smooth functioning of the Doric system of proportions—to him, a "machine à émouvoir," an emotion-arousing machine. To the Parthenon he devoted the last chapter of his first great book, Vers une architecture:

"The Greeks built temples on the Acropolis which answer to a single conception, and which have gathered up around them the desolate landscape and subjected it to the composition. So from all sides of the horizon the conception is unique. This is why no other works of architecture exist which have this grandeur. One can speak 'Doric' when man, by the loftiness of his views and by the complete sacrifice of accident, has attained the higher region of the mind: austerity."

16

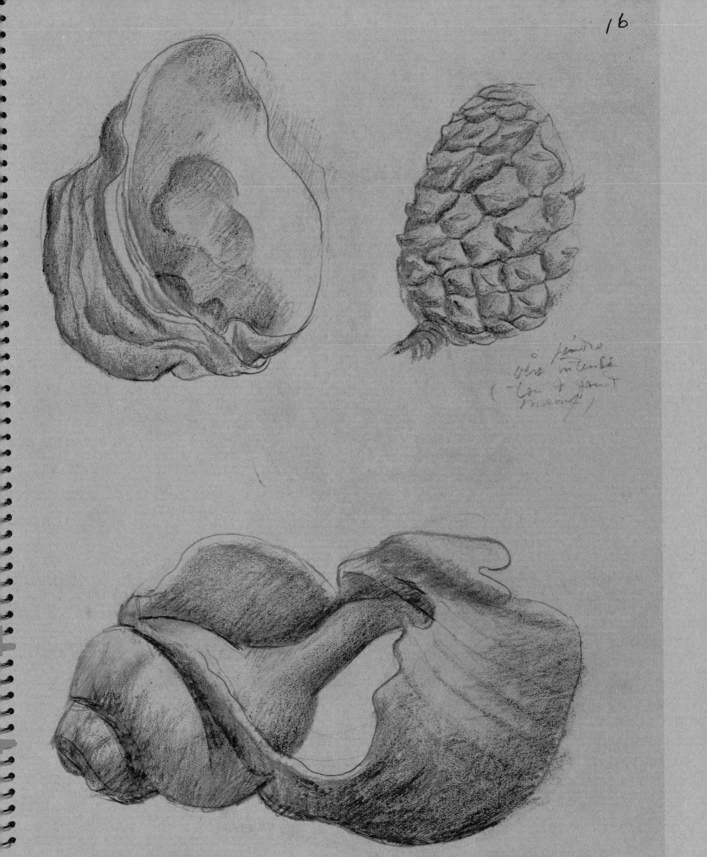

When Jeanneret arrived in Paris, though the Ecole des Beaux-Arts still controlled the general orientation of architecture, there were plenty of signs that things were about to change. To the great metal constructions of the late nineteenth century were now being added the first structures in reinforced concrete. If Art Nouveau architecture was already on the way out, a new generation was coming to the fore with Frantz Jourdain, François Le Cœur, Henri Sauvage, and above all Auguste Perret. Tony Garnier's designs for an Industrial City, though not yet very widely known, had just created a sensation. "When I went to Paris in 1908," Le Corbusier later confessed, "the Samaritaine of Frantz Jourdain already existed, but we thought it very witty at that time to make fun of its domes with their decorative ironwork, and we forgot to consider that its lateral façades were entirely in glass (the Centrosoyuz in Moscow was no more and no less)." He liked to recall, however, that he often went to look at the two houses Le Cœur had just built in rue Cassini: "I knew nothing more modern then." He entered Perret's office and worked under him for fifteen months. "In those years 1908-1909," he later wrote, "Perret played a heroic part in venturing to build with reinforced concrete, and in asserting, after de Baudot, that this method of construction would bring with it a new attitude to architecture. In the history of modern architecture Auguste Perret holds a very precise position, and a very high rank. He is a 'builder.' Whenever I talked about him in Germany in 1910 and declared that he alone at the time was moving in a new architectural direction, I was laughed at, disbelieved, and overruled: he was totally ignored.

◄ *Sketch of Sea Shells and Pine Cone, 1930. Pencil and color crayons on paper.*

Auguste Perret (1874-1954).
25 bis, rue Franklin in Paris,
Façade, 1902.

Une Villa
DE LE CORBUSIER
1916

Dans ses articles remarquables de l'*Esprit Nouveau*, Le Corbusier-Saugnier, architecte, avec modestie, ne s'est occupé que des rapports de l'ingénieur avec la construction moderne, afin de mettre en évidence les conditions primordiales de l'architecture : le jeu des formes dans l'espace, leur conditionnement par les procédés de construction. Il a montré que le calcul peut introduire à une grande architecture, que les moyens de construire actuels (financiers et techniques) offrent des ressources plus vastes que ceux des époques passées.

Le Corbusier sut, dans ses articles, lui artiste, faire momentanément abstraction des qualités de sensibilité qui font l'artiste, pour dégager, avant tout, les moyens de l'ingénieur,

His house in rue Franklin was denounced as Jugendstil because he covered it with faience. But that house was a manifesto... The Industrial City designs seem to have made an equally strong impression on Jeanneret: "Tony Garnier sensed that the birth of a new architecture was at hand, an architecture based on social factors. His plans show great ability... in them reigns the French planning skill." But "planning skill" was not the only thing that appealed to him here: like many others, then and later, he marveled at and profited by the profusion of new ideas and inventions of detail offered by Garnier's Cité Industrielle, an anticipation unique in the history of architecture.*

From Paris he went to Berlin and his stay there was no less fruitful. Here he worked under Peter Behrens, for whom, and for whose architecture, he felt little sympathy: he reproached him with trying to appear rather than to be. But he recognized in Behrens a new and authoritative creator of forms, the symmetrical and complementary counterpart of the "builder" he saw in Perret: a universal designer.

"*L'Esprit Nouveau,*" No. 6, page 679 :
Villa Schwob at La Chaux-de-Fonds, built by Le Corbusier in 1916.

François Le Cœur (1872-1934).
Artists' Studios, rue Cassini,
Paris, 1906.

Frantz Jourdain (1847-1935).
Samaritaine Department Store in Paris, 1905.

Tony Garnier (1869-1948).
Project for an Industrial City.
Apartment Blocks
in a Residential District, 1901-1904.

Behrens was equally at home in designing a page layout, publicity lettering, a lighting system or an industrial plant. In Berlin Jeanneret made his first acquaintance, through books, with the rationalist architecture of the Dutchman Berlage, in particular with his method of modular design. And in Berlin he discovered the work of Frank Lloyd Wright, revealed in 1910 to the younger European generation by an exhibition and two books. To Wright, Jeanneret owed above all a conception of the freedom of the plan quite different from the conception Perret had arrived at by the use of a reinforced concrete frame.

While Berlin and Paris mark the decisive stages of these prentice years, it would be a mistake to underestimate the influence of the contacts he had made in 1907 during a brief stay in Vienna, where he worked for Hoffmann.

FASSADE DES BÖRSENGEBÄUDES ZU AMSTERDAM
MIT EINGEZEICHNETEM SYSTEM. ENTW. H. P. BERLAGE

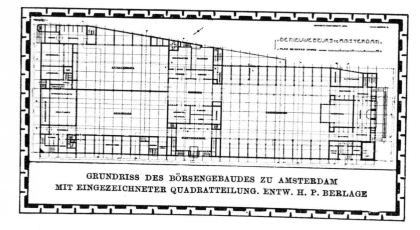

GRUNDRISS DES BÖRSENGEBAUDES ZU AMSTERDAM
MIT EINGEZEICHNETER QUADRATTEILUNG. ENTW. H. P. BERLAGE

H.P. Berlage (1856-1934).
Elevation and Plan of the Amsterdam
Stock Exchange, 1897-1903.

Frank Lloyd Wright (1869-1959).
Ward W. Willits House at Highland Park, Illinois, 1902.
Ink, watercolor and gouache on paper.

Peter Behrens (1868-1940). A.E.G. Factory for Small Motors, Brunnenstrasse, Berlin, 1910-1911.

*Josef Hoffmann (1870-1956).
Stoclet House in Brussels,
1906-1911.*

*Adolf Loos (1870-1933).
Steiner House in Vienna,
1910.*

The elegant spareness achieved by Josef Hoffmann, in reaction against the overblown Jugendstil of men like Olbrich, and the moral rigor with which Adolf Loos formulated the requirements of modern life and industrial production, both aroused his enthusiasm. In 1921, when he printed in L'Esprit Nouveau the French translation of Loos' famous article "Ornament and Crime," Jeanneret-Le Corbusier introduced the author in the warmest terms: "M. Loos is one of the precursors of the new spirit. As early as 1900, when enthusiasm for Art Nouveau was at its height, at a time of out and out decorativeness, of irrelevant intrusions of Art into everything, M. Loos, a man of clear and original views, began protesting against the futility of such trends. One of the first to sense the grandeur of industry and its contributions to aesthetics, he began to proclaim certain truths which still today seem revolutionary or paradoxical. In his own work, unfortunately too little known, he was the harbinger of a style which is only taking shape today."

A New Spirit

A great age has just begun.
A new spirit has come into being.

Still Life with a Pile of Dishes, 1920. Oil on canvas. Signed Jeanneret.

A NEW SPIRIT

WHEN Charles-Edouard Jeanneret finally settled in Paris, in 1917, he was already thirty years old. At that time Cubism was in its seventh year, but so far Le Corbusier would seem not to have given it the slightest attention. Nevertheless, it was in terms of Cubism that he elected to take up his own position, choosing the title *After Cubism* for the manifesto which he published, together with Amédée Ozenfant, to announce their first joint exhibition, held from December 1918 to January 1919.

By 1918, in fact, it was already abundantly clear that Cubism had completed that dislocation of the traditional concept of plastic space originally started by Manet and remorselessly pursued by others ever since. To many, it was equally evident that the succession to Cubism lay wide open. Many of the solutions proposed by its pioneers, and hastily canonized by its successors, were already felt to be compromises hard to justify. But the war scattered those who, from 1913-1914 onwards, had gauged the true dimensions of the event and had drawn the

necessary consequences. The noisy program of the Futurists, which had created such turmoil on the eve of the conflict, had now hung fire; the Section d'Or and Blauer Reiter groups had broken up, the Delaunays were isolated in Spain, while the Dutch and the Russians found themselves cut off from the world. As a result, in the atmosphere of uncertainty of the immediate post-war period, the balance sheet drawn up in a manifesto by two beginners was to find an unexpectedly loud echo. In it, Jeanneret and Ozenfant stressed the ethical value of the principles laid down by the initiators of Cubism. By reducing form to its geometrical—and hence intelligible—elements, by re-evaluating the notion of composition—that is, construction—Cubism had helped to set painting on the path of its true vocation once more. But the method of analysis it used had led to a splintering of form to which, despite its best efforts, it had failed to find a remedy. Even more serious in their eyes was the laxity displayed by Cubism in the application of the constructive principle. Beneath an appearance

◀ *Georges Braque (1882-1963). Man with a Pipe. Pasted paper and charcoal on Ingres paper.*

Page 36: Pablo Picasso (1881). Woman with a Guitar, 1914. Oil.

Page 37: Bottles and Glasses, 1922. Pencil and color crayons. Signed Jeanneret.

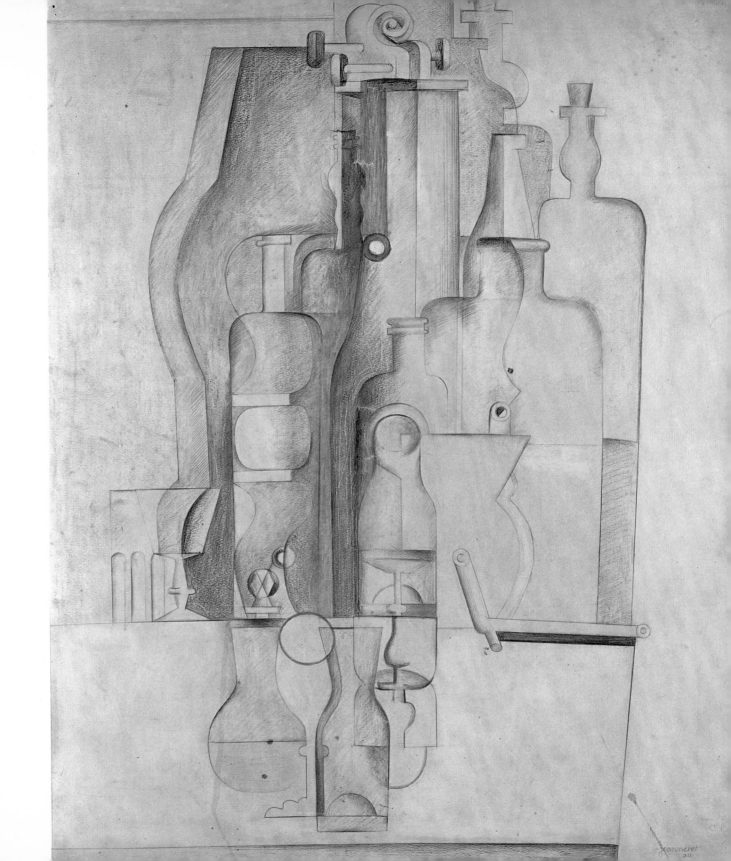

of austerity, it had in fact admitted all manner of decorative embellishment. From this they concluded that the new times demanded a spirit of exactitude of which Cubism had shown itself incapable.

However, important as the publication of *After Cubism* undoubtedly was, by reason of the unequivocal position adopted by its two authors, it was not until three years later that the decisive event intervened. In a series of articles which appeared in the review he had just founded with Ozenfant and Paul Dermée—*L'Esprit Nouveau*—Jeanneret-Le Corbusier extended his analysis of problems of painting to include an equally challenging examination of the contemporary state of the world of form. These articles made a considerable impact and immediately stamped the new review, together with *De Stijl*, as the most significant organ of the new post-Cubist avant-garde. In 1923, these articles were reprinted in *Vers une architecture*. In the same year Gropius, with his *Idee und Aufbau des Bauhauses*, published the manifesto in which he established in definitive form his own position, hitherto tinged by a somewhat confused romanticism, on the relation between artistic activity and industrial production.

On the left: Alexander Archipenko (1887-1964). ►
Man Standing, 1920. Stone.

On the right: Jacques Lipchitz (1891). ►
Sailor with a Guitar, 1917. Stone.

Ozenfant and Jeanneret in L'Esprit Nouveau *were among the first to call attention to the new sculpture of Lipchitz, Laurens and Archipenko who, instead of proceeding by combinations of masses, multiplied negative volumes, the voids produced by sunk carving, and even opened up holes in their statues. Jeanneret at once saw the significance of this step from the point of view of the new architectural space. In 1936 Le Corbusier pointed out that the full implications of their work had still not been grasped (they were not in fact to be grasped and developed until after the Second World War): "Following the Cubist revolt and revolution, we saw sculptors create 'perforated sculpture' because they realized that in this way it could be incorporated more multifariously into a site, a whole landscape, a whole room. These mathematical places are the very integral of the architecture of the new age, whose basic law is to be a palpitating, exact, efficient, simple, harmonious organism, with far-reaching intimations and radiating waves. It is safe to say that this sculpture is an unprecedented venture and that something new will come out of it."*

Henri Laurens (1885-1954).
Bottle of Rum, 1918. Wood.

With this, there had now been formulated all the essential themes of that "new spirit" which was very soon to manifest itself in architecture in the guise of what is generally termed the International Style.

It did not seem, *a priori*, as if the Cubist system of space construction could be applied to fields other than that of painting. Was not the problem posed by the Cubists precisely that of the total integration of the three-dimensional forms of sense experience within the two-dimensional universe of the canvas? Did not their system of figuration of the object by partial projections upon a series of superimposed planes denote the most radical attempt so far undertaken by Western schools of painting in their effort to reduce volume to surface? And yet, despite the purely pictorial orientation of their preoccupations, the Cubists in fact produced important suggestions for the organization of architectural space. In the first place, the simultaneous representation of the object from several angles implied at least a virtual mobility on the part of the spectator, who was henceforth permitted—nay, invited—to abandon the single viewpoint to which an age-old tradition had condemned him, and to move freely, at least in thought, around the object represented. Transposed to the plane of the practicable space of architecture, this new mobility made it possible to break with the classical system of static, purely visual, arrangements, composed in terms of axes and symmetries, and to endeavor to reintegrate within architecture the sum total of the complex experience of movement. Up to that time, only Frank Lloyd Wright had conceived

Walter Gropius (1883).
Spiral Staircase of the Administrative Office Building at the Werkbund Exhibition, Cologne, 1914.

of architecture in terms of movement on the part of the occupant, and even he had set out from totally different premises.

By multiplying the number of views taken of an object in order to acquire fuller cognizance of it, Cubism at the same time introduced a factor of relativity. By superimposing non-concordant, discontinuous images, it stripped the object of its opacity, its density, rendering it at once transparent and permeable to the medium which surrounds it, and with which it then engages in an interplay of unstable, shifting relations. It has long been realized that this bursting of the hitherto impenetrable outer covering of things, this reduction of the object to a transparent order, this copenetration of interior and exterior—that all this corresponded very closely to that experience of space which modern construction had already been proposing for several decades previously. It had in effect replaced the compact masses and stable volumes of traditional masonry by linear structures in which the copenetration of interior and exterior was realized in practice.

Mies van der Rohe (1886). Project for a Glass Skyscraper: View of the Model and Floor Plan, 1921.

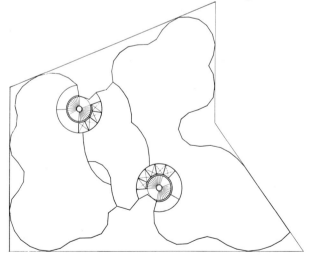

While the metal structural frame remains visible from the outside, the free form curvature of the glass envelope is calculated to make the most of the play of light and the reflective qualities of glass.

Richard Neutra (1892). Lovell House, Griffith Park, Los Angeles, 1927-1929.

In the years 1910-1930 glass architecture developed side by side with the new system of building with metal or reinforced concrete skeletons. Glass was handled in very different ways, depending on the time and place. In Germany, Expressionism laid stress on qualifying the light inside the building by means of colored glass, and on obtaining a play of external reflections by means of multifaceted prisms. This latter device had some influence on Mies van der Rohe's first skyscraper projects. Gropius, on the other hand, from his Alfeld factory to the Dessau Bauhaus, emphasized above all the pure transparency of the glass wall, which had been first utilized by Perret in the rue Ponthieu garage; later, in the church of Notre-Dame du Raincy, Perret made a point of breaking up its uniformity by the use of decorative concrete window grilles. In the United States, Holland and France, the glass wall was taken up more and more: Neutra's Lovell house and Pierre Chareau's Dalsace house (the latter slightly later than Le Corbusier's glass apartment house in Geneva, from which Chareau took many details) are particularly brilliant examples of architectural compositions from which stable volumes have been totally eliminated in favor of transparent or translucid planes fitted into strictly one-dimensional supporting elements.

In these houses the metallic frame of the glass wall forms a regular pattern capable of almost unlimited extension: at the Bauhaus it continues without a break around three sides of the building housing the collective workshops; the same is true of the Centrosoyuz. The appearance of this continuous network curiously coincides with the development in painting of the space-grid, whose first manifestations go back to the years 1914-1918. It was then, in reaction against the ambiguity of the multifocal system of Cubist space, that Mondrian began organizing the picture around an evenly distributed play of plus and minus signs which, from 1918 on, fell into a homogeneous grid covering the entire canvas. Paul Klee, in his Kairouan watercolors of 1914, likewise worked up the colored sectors into a scheme which, after 1918, took the form of a regular check pattern. At Zurich in 1915, Arp and Sophie Täuber, starting out from the latter's weaving designs, also arrived at check-pattern compositions. The check pattern played a large part in the exercises of the Vorkurs, or basic course, given at the Bauhaus by Johannes Itten. The mechanical screens of printer's plates were introduced about 1922-1924 by the Pole Berlewi in his "mecanofactures," in order to obtain a continuous vibration effect on the surface. Such animated patterns became a basic motif not only in industrialized construction (curtain walls, network structures) but in the researches of optical art.

◄ Pierre Chareau (1883-1950).
House of Dr Dalsace,
rue Saint-Guillaume, Paris:
Pivoting Doors
of Plate Glass and Metal, 1931.

Piet Mondrian (1872-1944). ►
Composition, 1919. Oil on canvas.

Paul Klee (1879-1940).
Static and Dynamic Gradation, 1923. Oil.

Finally, by reducing the complexity of the forms of sense experience to a limited number of geometric elements, Cubism had facilitated the assimilation of that formal language, shorn of all accidental detail, which was the specific of that construction.

The liberation of space which Cubism had accomplished in the sphere of the plastic arts (the experiments of the painters were soon followed by those of sculptors: Duchamp-Villon, Lipchitz, Archipenko, Laurens) thus opened up vast horizons in architecture also: mobilization of space, transparency of "open" structures, geometrization of the formal elements. All of these were demands implicit in the new architectural ethic which had been evolving since the turn of the century, but which the example of Cubism alone enabled architects to assimilate aesthetically. This shock was thus necessary before architecture could break free from the inertia of a stereometric way of thinking, or assimilate the machine aesthetic, which constituted an essential stage in its reintegration within the life of the modern world.

However, pursuing still further its analysis of the two essential contributions of Cubism—the dynamic continuity of space and the notion of the plastic element—the current of thought originally provoked by Cubism was soon destined to overtake it. Indeed, it was around these two themes that there developed, "after Cubism," that great debate which culminated in the definition of utterly new plastic and architectural concepts, and it was within the context of this debate that the resounding intervention of Le Corbusier was situated.

Criticism was directed at once against the treatment of the plastic element, which the Cubists had failed to strip of all figurative value, and against the construction of space by fragmentation of form, which contradicted the suggestion of movement inherent in the multiplication of viewpoints. Such criticism was levelled, either in the name of plastic purity (by Mondrian and Malevich, for instance) or in the name of the dynamism of machine civilization, whose brutally contrasting rhythms and colors Cubism, by a strange paradox, had proved incapable of translating. The motif of simultaneity, developed on the eve of the war by Orphism and Futurism and reinterpreted in the immediate post-war years by the Dadaists in their *collages*, found a notable echo amongst the Constructivists of Central and Eastern Europe. In order to assert the omnipresence of the machine, they went to the length of introducing real movement into some of their plastic constructions (Rodchenko, Gabo, Moholy-Nagy) and even into their architectural projects (Tatlin). Amongst these experiments, particular importance attaches to certain schools for working out elementarist design—introduced, for a brief period, in the "Vkhutemas" and subsequently continued, for fourteen years, in the Bauhaus founded by Gropius.

In the course of this debate, often confused, but extraordinarily fertile, new hypotheses were formulated concerning the nature of plastic and architectural space: the afocal space-grid, explored by Mondrian, Arp, or Klee; the space-field of energies, already revealed before the war by Kandinsky, Delaunay, and Kupka, and transposed into three dimensions by Gabo and Pevsner; the space-time of shifting light, heralded by Moholy-Nagy and reproduced in the experimental films of Viking Eggeling and Hans Richter.

Walter Gropius (1883). The Bauhaus, Dessau: ▶
General View of the Entrance, 1925-1926.

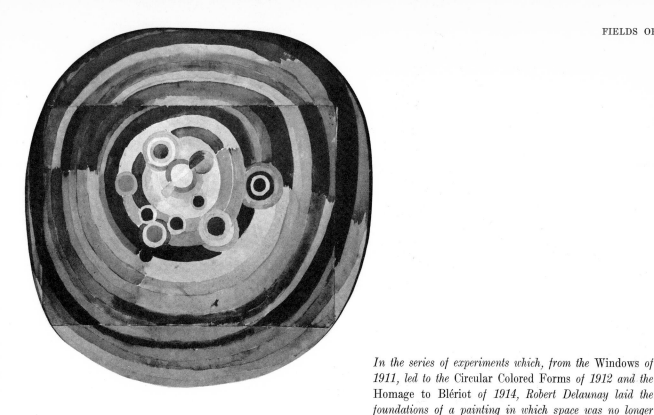

Robert Delaunay (1885-1941).
Football, 1918. Watercolor on pasted paper and cardboard.
Sketch for the set of a ballet planned with Léonide Massine.

◄ Wassily Kandinsky (1866-1944).
In the Black Square, 1923. Oil on canvas.

In the series of experiments which, from the Windows of 1911, led to the Circular Colored Forms of 1912 and the Homage to Blériot of 1914, Robert Delaunay laid the foundations of a painting in which space was no longer treated as a construction resulting from the combination of independent forms or based on homogeneous patterning: space now was pure radiance born of the interaction of colors. "Space, form, color, light are one" (Georg Schmidt). The picture surface was constellated with foci around which space was organized in concentric zones of unequal density. The space of the famous abstractions painted by Kandinsky in the same pre-war years answers to a very similar topological conception; one finds this space again, drained of all expressionism, in his Bauhaus canvases. In sculpture, certain works of Archipenko and Lipchitz also seem to imply a non-homogeneous structure of space, alternately contracting and expanding. Nodes and surfaces non-developable in the plane became after 1925 the fundamental elements of the plastic idiom of Gabo and Pevsner. It was about this time that curved surfaces began to be used and developed in reinforced concrete structures (Freyssinet). Le Corbusier took a keen interest in this from the time L'Esprit Nouveau was launched, and in the Ronchamp chapel he used curved surfaces of reinforced concrete with a poetry and daring still unsurpassed.

Antoine Pevsner (1884-1962). Projection into Space, 1927. Bronze.

The deeper study and further development of these hypotheses—delayed by the new dispersion which followed the advent of National-Socialism in Germany and by the generally retrograde trends of the 1930's—did not finally take place until thirty years later, with the revival, following the wave of lyrical abstractionism and informalism, of the underlying themes of constructive abstraction.

With Neo-Plasticism and Suprematism on the one side and Constructivism on the other, the position of Le Corbusier in this debate was an original and, for all his peremptory manner of diction, a highly differentiated one. In common with Mondrian and Malevich, as well as Gleizes and Juan Gris, he shared the demand for severity in the organization of space —the need to retain, beyond the accidental, only the mathematical element—and went on to postulate the purely spiritual vocation of art in the following words: "Modern painting has abandoned the wall, the tapestry, the decorative urn, and has withdrawn into a frame. Nurtured, replete with facts, far removed from the distracting influence of figuration, it lends itself to meditation. Art no longer tells a tale, it makes one think."

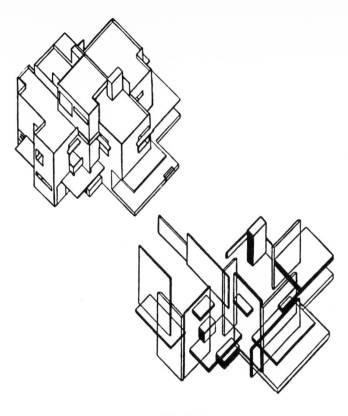

Theo van Doesburg (1883-1931)
and Cornelis van Eesteren (1897).
Two Studies for a Dwelling House, one with opaque,
the other with transparent volumes, 1923.

In modern art theory the introduction of the idea of an "element," in the sense of a simple geometric form, goes back to the reinterpretation given by Cézanne and Seurat of certain themes of the classical tradition. The term itself does not appear to have been used by artists and theorists before the end of the First World War. Theo van Doesburg alone expressly designated his painting as "elementarist," but for all the artists who followed the line of Constructivism or "concrete art" the quest for the elementary, always conceived in geometric terms, played a decisive part—though this quest also had its place in a much larger movement in which the psychoanalytical and surrealistic investigation of the unconscious may be taken to represent the opposite aspect.

Contributing factors in the success of this idea were the geometric design of the forms born of industry and also certain philosophical and theosophical speculations. But perhaps the main reason for its success was the hope it inspired of re-establishing a unity of style and design in the arts and architecture. For the element facilitated the passage from one register to another, a facility eagerly seized on by certain artists of the De Stijl group and by Malevich in passing by imperceptible transitions from the level of plastic figuration to that of inhabitable space: "Constructivism," as Lissitzky put it, "is the way station on the line to architecture." The influence of the elementarist aesthetic on International Style architecture was considerable; it can be seen in Mies van der Rohe, Gropius and Le Corbusier. Both in his painting and his architecture Le Corbusier relied heavily on the notion of the "element" as well as on the related but less abstract and more human ideas of the "standard" and the "organ." Among the different approaches to elementarism, Purism was the only one to reject pure abstraction. "Primary forms and colors," wrote Ozenfant and Jeanneret in L'Esprit Nouveau, *"have standard properties (universal properties permitting the creation of a transmissible plastic language). But the use of primary forms does not enable the artist to put the spectator into the desired mathematical state. For that, he has to call on associations of natural or artificial forms, and in choosing them the criterion is the degree of selection at which certain elements have arrived (natural selection and mechanical selection). The purist element resulting from the purifying of the standard forms is not a copy but a creation whose aim is to materialize the object in all its generality and its invariability. The purist elements then may be likened to words with a well-defined meaning: the purist syntax is the application of constructive and modular means: it is the application of the laws governing the picture space. A picture is a whole (unit): a picture is an artificial formation which, by suitable means, should aim at the objectification of a whole 'world.' One can make an art of allusions, an art of fashion, based on surprise and the conventions of a coterie. Purism aims at an art making use of plastic constants, avoiding conventions, addressing itself first and foremost to the universal properties of the senses and the mind."*

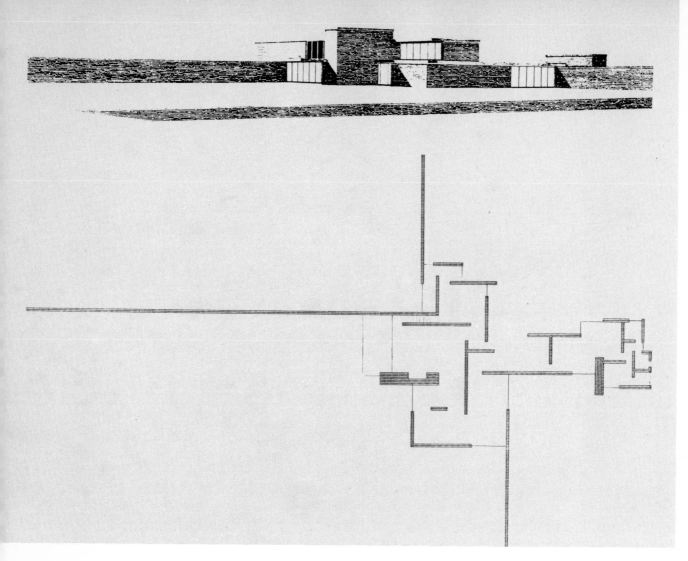

Mies van der Rohe (1886). Project and Plan for a Brick Country House, 1923.

Kasimir Malevich (1878-1935). House of the Future, 1924. Pen and ink on cardboard. ▶

The projects of Mies van der Rohe in which the Neo-Plastic influence is most conspicuous are two country houses, one in brick, the other in concrete. It is worth comparing these projects with the Suprematist sketches of Malevich. The latter, as early as 1914, entitled one of his canvases "Houses under Construction," the implication being that in the art of the future there would be a natural transition from painting to architecture. Malevich later drew up many projects for "Planits" or dwellings of the future. His designs and models, however, did not go beyond a rather summary indication of volumes. The bird's-eye view shows to advantage the pure, uncluttered surface of the terrace-roof, from which chimneys have been eliminated, for the "Planits" were to be heated by electricity—at that time a distinctly futuristic note.

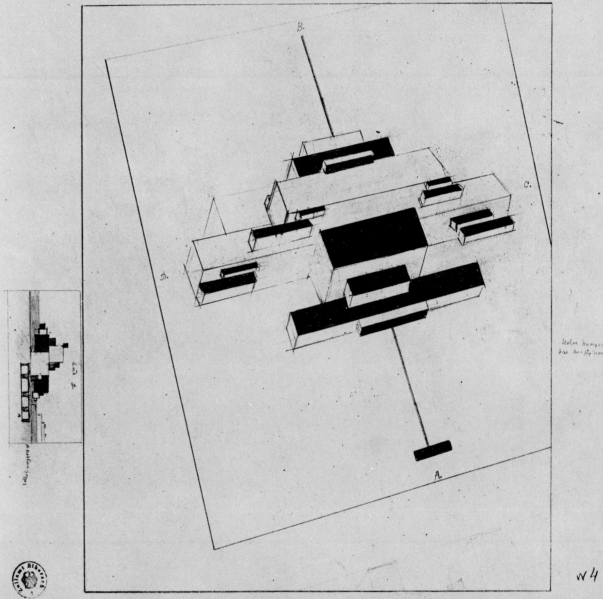

"Уновис"
Будущие "планиты" /дома/ землянитов /людей/

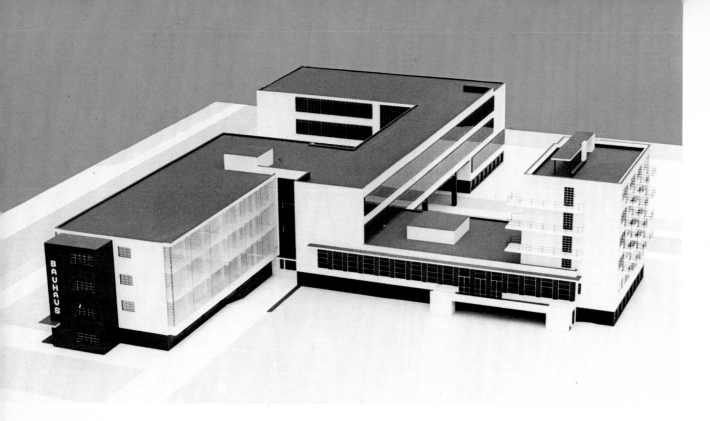

Walter Gropius (1883). Bird's-Eye View of the Model for the Dessau Bauhaus, 1926.

At the same time, though Le Corbusier was apparently on good terms with Mondrian, and especially with Theo van Doesburg, he unequivocally took his distance from Neo-Plasticism and Elementarism when he refused to reject the physical reality of forms or to reduce the wealth of concrete plastic situations to the uniformity of an abstract system of signs. "Geometry," he was to say forty years later, defining in a word the nature of his disagreement with the De Stijl group, "geometry is not in the wrist, it is in the weighing."

This determination to preserve the weight of things, to retain their specific density, led Le Corbusier and Ozenfant, during the first phase of their Purist researches, to effect what might at first sight seem to represent a retreat in relation to Cubism. Yet although, temporarily at any rate, they renounced transparency and laid the emphasis on half-relief, this was not done with any intention of reverting to realism, to the anecdotic or decorative description of the real, but rather, by affirming the "plastic continuum," to guarantee the complete control of the relations linking the elements of the composition to one another. This was neither realism nor empiricism, but rather a desire to intellectualize the creative process, no whit less rigorous than that of De Stijl. The viewpoints were no longer to be combined in haphazard fashion, as in Cubist paintings,

George Vantongerloo (1886-1965). Construction of Volume Relations, 1921. Mahogany.

El Lissitzky (1890-1941). Proun I D, 1919. Oil on canvas.

The articulation of the different units of the Bauhaus —clearly visible only in bird's-eye view—situates this masterpiece of twentieth century architecture at the meeting point of the two main currents of European "elementarism": Neo-Plasticism and Suprematism (whose manifestoes in fact were published in the series of Bauhaus Books). As for his "Prouns," Lissitzky himself saw them as standing midway between plastic figuration and an architectural utopia. What he meant them to suggest, he said, was "a world of crystalline organisms floating in a visually infinite space."

Vladimir Tatlin (1885-1956).
Project for a Monument
to the Third International,
1919-1920.

Naum Gabo (1890).
Column, 1923.
Plastic, metal and wood.

From Apollinaire to Mayakovsky, from Léger to Marcel Duchamp, from Le Corbusier to Moholy-Nagy, from Gropius to Max Ernst and even Klee (who painted a Twittering Machine), there was general agreement among the avant-garde all over Europe that it was imperative for art to take into account the omnipresent reality of the machine in the modern world. There were great differences of opinion, however, on the position and significance to be accorded it. All those members of the Constructivist movement who had come under Futurist influence took over directly the forms, fittings and materials of the machine (in particular polished metal surfaces), and even the working of it (which after all is its essence), introducing actual movement into their works. Dada took it up as an instrument well suited to poking ridicule not only at traditional, pre-Machine Age art but at the machine itself which, in the mechanical drawings of Picabia, parodies its own functioning and emphasizes the vanity of all rational activity: Marcel Duchamp's Large Glass is the ironic rejoinder to Tatlin's projected monument to the Third International. Others, like Gropius and Le Corbusier, realized that the growth and spread of mass production would require of modern man new disciplines, a new outlook, a new way of thinking. Issue No. 21 of L'Esprit Nouveau illustrated the "formation of the modern vision" by comparing the constructions of (among others) Moholy-Nagy and Medunetzky with the Purist canvases of Jeanneret and Ozenfant. But, for Le Corbusier, the machine remained essentially a lesson in method and a begetter of new standards. In his eyes, the "lyricism of the new age" had nothing to do with a Machine Age romanticism: "The machine has been made into a new god, whereas it should be seen only as an inevitable product of human activity forging its tools. As we have shown, it is a product answering more exactly to the laws of nature than did those created by the craftsman. The machine is above all in keeping with our new social being, the token of the higher law determining our civilization, the law of economy... Economy, Purity, key of the new spirit."

Laszlo Moholy-Nagy (1895-1946).
Light-Space Modulator, 1922-1930.
Motor-driven construction of metal, plastic and wood.

Fernand Léger (1881-1955). The Deck of the Tugboat, 1920. Oil on canvas.

but were to correspond exclusively to the most artificial angles of vision, i.e. elevation and plan. At the same time, the organization of the surface was submitted to the objective control of regulating grids based on mathematical ratios and simple geometric figures. "Geometry is in the weighing..." Like Mondrian or Kandinsky during the Bauhaus years, Le Corbusier saw, in the construction of the canvas, a problem of equilibrium; like them, moreover, he refused to solve this problem according to the traditional formulas of a realistic repartition of the centers of gravity. Unlike the pioneers of abstraction, however, he conceived of this equilibrium as representing the balancing of plastic objects which would retain their own density, a density such that, in relation to his early Purist paintings, one may freely speak of architecture in the truest sense of the term.

It was likewise the demands of a fundamentally architectural approach that determined the positions Le Corbusier took up in relation to the problem of construction and that of the machine. His positions here were at once close to, yet very different from, those of countless movements which grew up in the wake of Futurism, fired by the enthusiasm for machine civilization. From time to time, he contributed to Lissitzky's review, *Object*, yet at the same period he was to affirm: "Art has no business to resemble a machine (error of Constructivism)." In the same series of articles in *L'Esprit Nouveau* in which he had declared architecture to be "pure creation of the mind," Le Corbusier exalted in lyrical terms the moral qualities, the healthful and joyful attributes, of the engineer. The airplane—the "flying machine"— provided him with an example of a "well posed problem," by which he meant a problem posed in radically new terms, just as he wished to see posed

Above: Francis Picabia (1878-1953).
Universal Prostitution, 1916.
Pen and ink and show card color on cardboard.

Below: Marcel Duchamp (1887-1968).
The Bride Stripped Bare by Her Bachelors, Even
(The Large Glass), lower part, 1915-1923.

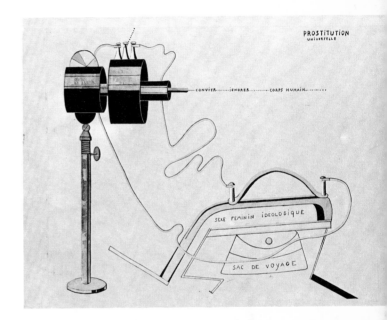

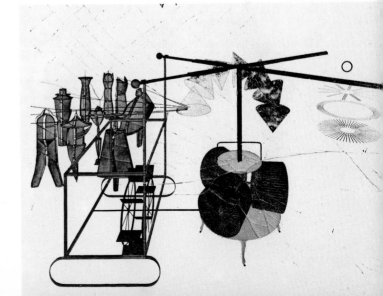

Amédée Ozenfant (1886-1966). Still Life with a Glass of Red Wine, 1921. Oil.

Still Life with Various Objects. Oil on canvas. Signed Jeanneret 1924.

the problem of the house—the "living-machine." In a series of parallel settings, such as a Soviet producer of the silent-film age would not have disavowed, Le Corbusier set off Bramante's loggias against American factories, the Parthenon against modern sports cars. Yet, however provocative these associations were designed to be, it was not Le Corbusier's intention to accentuate the opposition of forms in the spirit of Futurism, but rather to affirm the continuity of a spirit which had deserted architecture, and whose mantle was now being taken over by the art of the engineer. With reference to the new forms created by the machine (in this instance to the cabin of one of the first passenger airplanes), he noted that "this is not a grammar of forms, but simply, in a domain other than that of architecture, a state of harmonious agreement between nature and human workmanship."

This comment helps us to understand the famous remark in *Vers une architecture*: "Architecture is in the telephone and in the Parthenon, how comfortable it would feel in our houses!" The Parthenon and the telephone were in fact neither antagonistic nor interchangeable but, as elements of the research that was to lead "towards an architecture," complementary. The specific problems of architecture, which the example of the engineer's way of thinking should enable one to formulate in terms conforming to the demands of the "new spirit" —these problems lay beyond the sphere of construction. Just as he refused, with the Futurists, to reject *en bloc* the heritage of the past, so Le Corbusier, with a degree of rationalism, refused to equate architecture with construction. No sooner had he cited the engineers as a model than he abruptly took his distance from them: "Art has no business to resemble a machine." On the one hand, he retained the analogy of the machine, which he did much to publicize, in word and image, and which was to prove a source of countless misunderstandings; on the other, faced with the demands of reason which alone governed the process of construction, he stuck out for the rights of that "passion" out of which architecture, as "pure creation of the mind," was born.

Living-Machines

To put it in a nutshell:
we must have plenty of room in order
to live in full daylight,
so that the "animal" in us
won't feel cooped up,
so that it can move about,
have space around it and in front of it.

House built at the Weissenhof Exhibition at Stuttgart, 1927. East Front.

Jeanneret House in Paris, 1923. Interior.

MASS-PRODUCED HOUSES

More than the example of 25 bis, rue Franklin, in Paris, which housed Perret's offices during Le Corbusier's stay there in 1908, it seems to have been the inspiration of industrial buildings that suggested to him the principle of the "Dom-ino" system of 1914. For it was in the field of industry that reinforced concrete had begun, even before the First World War, to be a serious rival to the steel framework used hitherto. But the extension of such a system to the building of individual houses (the Dom-ino system was conceived with a view to the rapid reconstruction of the devastated towns of Flanders) could be justified economically only on the basis of mass production. It was in fact a system of prefabrication that Le Corbusier proposed, both for the elements of the framework and for the fittings. True, the idea of prefabrication had been in the air for some years. So far, however, and for a long time to come, prefabrication was regarded purely as a means of reducing building costs. By contrast, Le Corbusier from the very first drew conclusions of tremendous architectural and social significance, and these he was to extend even to the sphere of town-planning.

The first of these conclusions was paradoxical: for him, the industrialization of a building should enable its future occupants to participate actively, not only in the conception, but also in the construction, of their home. In his eyes, the resort to modern methods of organizing production had nothing in common with technical perfectionism. Technology was of value only to the extent that—so far from imposing new servitudes on man and condemning him to the role of passive onlooker—it helped to stimulate his initiative and took on a truly liberating mission.

In the Dom-ino system, the freeing of individual initiative was made possible by the severing of the time-honored link that existed between construction and architecture. In fact, the "column and slab" system ensured the independence of the architectural element in relation to the structural one: since the interior partitions were no longer load-bearing, they no longer need to be exactly superimposed from one story to the next, but could be freely disposed of at will. The eternal conflict of wall and window was also solved. Yet, no less than this newly won freedom, Le Corbusier emphasized the factor of unity, the "architectural assurance" created by this system: "despite the individual nature of each initiative applied, the technical process itself provided an underlying unity and lent the villages reconstructed in this way an element of architectural assurance..."

This assurance, this unity, was considered by Le Corbusier from two angles: on the one hand, the same process of construction was applicable to all types of house, whether luxury or ultra-simple, and so guaranteed the same fundamental freedom to both; on the other, it provided a sound basis for tackling the problem of group settlements, i.e. urban schemes: "The unity of the constructional elements is a guarantee of beauty; architectural diversity is ensured by the process of allotment leading to large-size schemes, the true rhythms of architecture." Far from eliminating architecture, the industrialization of construction provided architecture with the instrument which would enable it to fulfill its true vocation: the satisfaction of the needs of the user and the planning of urban settlements.

"The example of the airplane shows us how a problem, once properly stated, finds its solutions; to wish to fly like a bird was to state the problem in wrong terms, and Ader's bat never got off the ground. But to invent a flying machine, with no harking back to anything divorced from pure mechanics—in other words, to look for an elevating force and a means of propulsion—was to state the problem in its proper form. Within less than ten years, everyone was able to fly... Now let us face the problem of the living-machine; and let us shut our eyes to everything that has existed hitherto."

"Living-machine": first launched in 1921 in *L'Esprit Nouveau*, the term scandalized people. The scandal lay in the fact that, like the airplane, the house was here treated as an entirely new problem, was invented afresh exclusively in terms of a civilization that was still rejected by the vast majority of opinion: on the one hand, technical possibilities, such as those offered by construction in reinforced concrete;

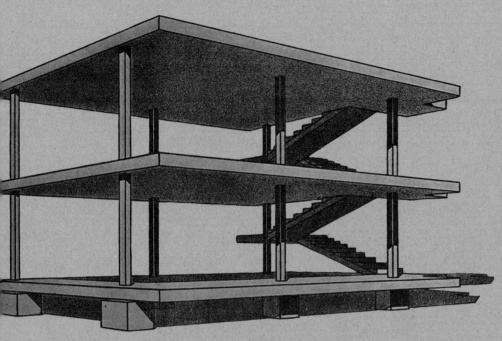

*Standard Column
and Slab Structure
for Mass-produced
Dom-ino Houses, 1914.*

*Framework of House A
at Weissenhof, 1927.*
▼

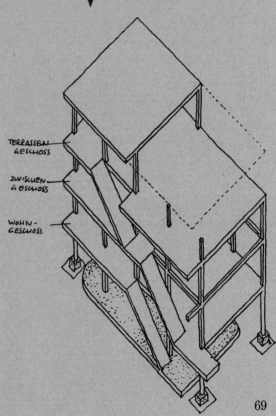

Le Corbusier worked out his Dom-ino housing scheme in the autumn of
1914 as a quick and inexpensive means of rebuilding the devastated towns
and villages of Flanders. He described it as follows: "So we designed a
structural system, a frame, completely independent of the functions of the
plan of the house: this frame simply supports the flooring and the staircase. It is made of standard elements which can be fitted together, thus
permitting a great diversity in the grouping of the houses... At the request
of the town-planner or customer, such frames, oriented and grouped, can be
delivered by a manufacturer anywhere in the country.

"It then remained to fit up a home inside these frames... We conceived
the idea of a firm, an affiliate of the first, which would sell all the elements
required to equip the house, everything, that is, which can be manufactured,
mass-produced in standard sizes, and meet the various needs of a rational
installation: windows, doors, standard casings serving as cupboards and
forming part of the dividing walls... Since the Dom-ino framework bore
the loads, the walls and partitions could be made of any material."

The Dom-ino system was neither the first nor the most perfected of the prefabricated housing schemes devised during the pioneer period of the history
of reinforced concrete. It was, however, the one which from the outset was
designed in the broadest perspective of architecture and town-planning.

Mass-produced Dom-ino Houses, 1914-1915.

Mass-produced Dom-ino Houses, 1915.

The Dom-ino system provided Le Corbusier with an instrument for the "occupation of space," as he later put it, one that left plenty of scope for the play of his imagination, which bore not so much on the creation of forms (as has been too often assumed) as of spatial situations. While he was always keenly interested in the new technical developments of construction, Le Corbusier kept all his life to the system of the structural frame or skeleton. So it is fitting to begin this survey of his "patient search"—as he himself began the edition of his Complete Works—with a tribute to this technique which in his hands proved so fruitful.

In the building projects which, between 1915 and 1920, followed the Dom-ino system (none of which was executed), we already find several of the characteristic elements of the "living-machines" of the decade 1920-1930, in particular the ribbon window and the terrace-roof, and even the living room with a double floor height. But what chiefly interested him at that time, even more than the treatment of the envelope or the freedom of interior organization made possible by the linear frame, was the problem of the grouping of the cells or rooms, which he envisaged as yet only as a horizontal juxtaposition of individual units.

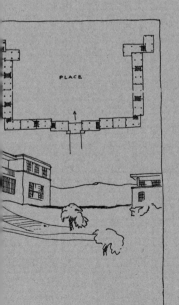

*Project for a ▶
Seaside Villa
for Paul Poiret,
1916.*

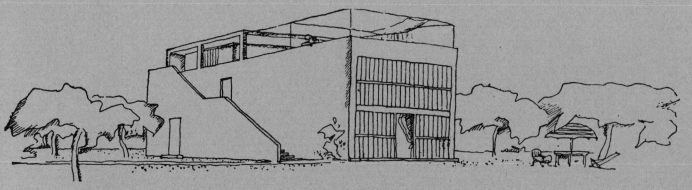

Citrohan House, first project, 1920.

It was not until 1920-1922, with the so-called Citrohan houses, that Le Corbusier squarely tackled—and solved in a revolutionary way—the problem of the room layout, by systematically setting off a large-sized living room, with a double floor height, against adjoining rooms and service premises arranged on several levels. The Citrohan House No. 2, a model of which was exhibited in Paris at the 1922 Salon d'Automne along with a diorama of his Contemporary City for Three Million Inhabitants, represents the first complete prototype of the "living-machine" independent of its site and capable of being adapted to almost any plot of ground. Le Corbusier built such a house for the first time at Stuttgart in 1927 (see pages 87-88).

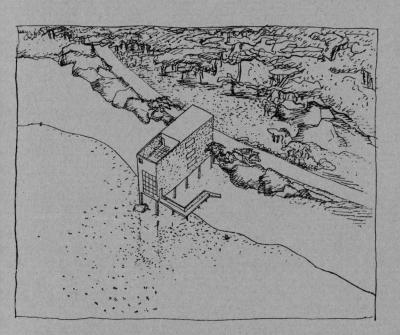

Citrohan House, project for a seaside villa on the French Riviera, 1922-1927.

on the other, economic imperatives, inasmuch as the ground space and the building space available had meanwhile become rare and costly. "There must be a reaction against the old type of house, with its misuse of space... Since the price of a building has quadrupled, we must reduce by half the claims of architecture as conceived hitherto, and at least by another half the cubic space of the houses... A house, like a motor-car, conceived and fitted out like a bus or a ship's cabin... Railway carriages, limousines have proved... that space can be calculated down to the nearest cubic centimeter." The reader will note that the comparisons are given systematically in terms of moving vehicles, never in terms of architectural precedents. In other words, it was less a problem of rectifying the dimensions or of revising the layout of buildings in terms of the real needs of contemporary man than of introducing a "new spirit" in order to tackle the problem of the house as such. Referring, in 1921, to the transportable houses mass-produced by the airplane constructor, Gabriel Voisin, Le Corbusier wrote that, in order to live in such houses, "one must have the mind of a sage and be animated by a new spirit." Again, in 1929, in reference to his own houses in the Weissenhof, he was to remark: "...implicit in this manifestation is *a moral attitude*, which explains the violent nature of the innumerable protests raised."

In Perret's offices in rue Franklin, Le Corbusier had witnessed how the use of a reinforced concrete framework made it possible to raise the optical center of gravity of a multistory building above ground level. Furthermore, Tony Garnier's industrial city had fired him with the dream of freeing buildings completely from the soil, so enabling pedestrians to pass unhampered across the entire city at street level.

◄ *Citrohan House, project for a villa in Paris, 1922-1927.*

Cook House at Boulogne-sur-Seine, 1926. Free-Standing Support or Stilt (pilotis).

As for the use of *pilotis*, or stilts, most critics have tended to emphasize that, by separating buildings completely from the ground, they lead to a considerable saving in excavation work and enable the living quarters to be arranged in more healthy fashion. In reality, the use of *pilotis*, by creating two continuous superimposed zones—one at ground level, for purposes of circulation, which is no longer limited by the alignment of the houses; the other, above this, for living quarters—posed the principle of a complete redistribution in the three dimensions of architectural space and urban space. Thus, the "living-machine" at once emerges as a machine for assisting traffic or, to use an expression later coined by Le Corbusier, as an "instrument of urban renovation." In place of the traditional concept of a "front" (façade), facing the main stream of traffic, and a "back," confined within the narrow limits of a courtyard, the "living-machine"—with its division into a "ground level" and an "upper level"—in effect introduced a clear-cut distinction between the two major functions of the city: exchange and intercourse on the one hand, living and accommodation on the other.

"The plan is inverted; one turns one's back on the street and looks towards the light." However, this inversion of the plan would not be complete unless the house, once detached from the soil, were at the

*Swiss Pavilion at the Cité Universitaire, Paris, 1930-1932.
Free-Standing Supports (pilotis).*

*Among the architectural devices introduced by Le Corbusier,
probably none has been more widely taken up and used than
the free-standing support (pilotis). For decades now it has
been a standard, indeed a stereotyped, feature of modern
buildings, or of buildings that want to seem modern. With
Le Corbusier himself, however, the pilotis, both in its underlying principle and in the forms it took, was a complex
reality in constant evolution: it provides a perfect example
of the way in which his faculty of invention was continually
intervening in his work. It is rare indeed for any invention
of his to be the fruit of a single intuition, to take at once a
definitive form. Even in the case of those elements which
he called standards, the initial invention provided merely
the point of departure for a series of re-elaborations and
reinventions which, from the initial premises, draw different
and sometimes contradictory meanings: it is this perpetual
reviewing and stating of a given problem that Le Corbusier
called his "patient search," and that he opposed to passive,
gratuitous, unfruitful illumination. At first the pilotis
was but an undifferentiated part of the structural frame;
soon, becoming visible as a result of the suppression of the
curtain-wall, it ceased to be treated as a simple, unexpressive*

Apartment Block (Unité d'Habitation) at Marseilles, 1945-1952. Free-Standing Supports (pilotis).

linear support and asserted itself as a plastic reality, if not independent, at least strongly individualized: the Marseilles apartment block marks the furthest point reached in this direction. In his later blocks, the pilotis, once linear and recently three-dimensional, now became a plane element. This reduction from pillar to slab of course meant a saving in costs, but there were also aesthetic reasons for it: the thin upright slabs of the pilotis extended down to the ground the verticals formed by the upright side-panels of the loggias, and thus fitted harmoniously into the overall surface pattern of the building. At Chandigarh, in the Palace of Justice and the Assembly Hall, the pilotis undergo a final metamorphosis comparable to that of the sun-breaks in the "light-wall" of the Ronchamp chapel. They no longer perform the function for which they were originally designed (which was, to lift the building off the ground). Serving simply to support a parasol roof, they are justified at Chandigarh only as purely poetic elements.

Assembly Hall at Chandigarh, 1950-1957. Free-Standing Supports (pilotis).

same time to be freed of the heavy load of the roof. Now, the system of reinforced concrete framework and slabs in fact provided, in the form of the roof-garden, just this chance to reconquer "the most precious space of all, the space beneath the sun." The terrace-roof, originally justified, in the Schwob House, on practical grounds (drawing off of rain water and melting snow towards the interior), had by 1922 become a practical proposition. Well away from traffic, it offered the ideal place for play and relaxation; it made it possible to introduce not only the sun but all nature once more into the daily life of the town-dweller; it let in light, by means of saw-tooth roofs or skylights, to the very heart of a building. No longer gripped in the vice represented by ground and roof, the living-machine could be freely situated in space. For Le Corbusier, the independence thus gained in relation to the street was an essential conquest, no less so than the overall gain of ground space and roof space which it entailed. These new conquests made it possible to define afresh the relation of the cell to its environment; the role of architecture was extended naturally to include town-planning, and town-planning in three dimensions.

But the "liberating potential" inherent in technical progress also provided other possibilities, including the free organization of the interior space and so the ability to project town-planning into the very heart of architecture. Le Corbusier did not at once discover all the possibilities offered by the "free plan"; these were revealed to him gradually, along with the first-hand experience acquired from the houses he was to build from 1922 onwards. In the initial phase (Dom-ino system, Schwob House), the replacement of load-bearing walls by pillars forming pin-point support was regarded only from the economy angle:

From the Citrohan house to the Villa Savoye, Le Corbusier designed many variations on the theme of the freedom of the plan, permitting the utmost variety in the arrangement of the rooms. All these projects were based on the column and slab structure derived from his Dom-ino system; the most modest, like the 1924 project for "artisans' houses," are by no means the least ingenious. It is interesting to compare the two very different examples of masterly house design illustrated here, the Villa at Carthage and the Villa Savoye. Quite apart from the contrasting modes of composition (which Le Corbusier seemed deliberately to emphasize), the two houses are characterized by the use of the same counterpoint between the frame on the one hand and the envelope and the internal divisions on the other.

The Villa Savoye achieves an interpenetration not only of internal and external spaces, but above all of different floor levels; this, for reasons that need not concern us here, is quite lacking at Carthage. The counterpoint between frame and envelope is a constant feature of Le Corbusier's architectural designs, appearing even in such later works as the Assembly Hall at Chandigarh and in the unexecuted projects for the Governor's Palace at Chandigarh and a Congress Hall at Strasbourg.

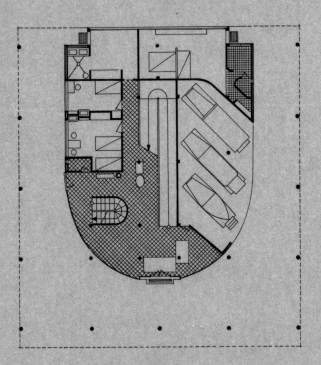

Villa Savoye at Poissy, 1929-1931.
Plan of the ground floor, with driveway and garage under
the stilts (pilotis), service premises, and guest rooms.

Villa at Carthage, 1929.
Plan of the ground floor.

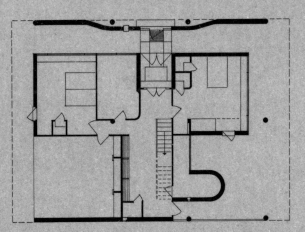

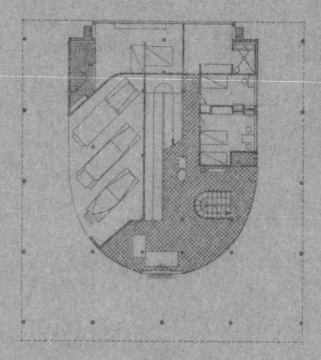

Villa Savoye at Poissy, 1929-1931.
Plan of the ground floor, with driveway and garage under
the stilts (pilotis), service premises, and guest rooms.

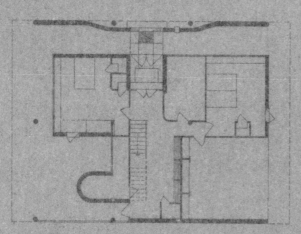

Villa at Carthage, 1929.
Plan of the ground floor.

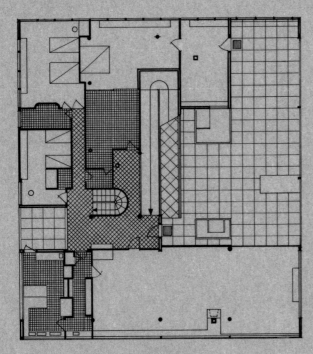

Villa Savoye at Poissy, 1929-1931.
Plan of the living quarters on the first floor, with terrace-roof.

Villa at Carthage, 1929.
Plan of the first floor.

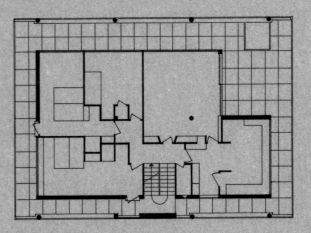

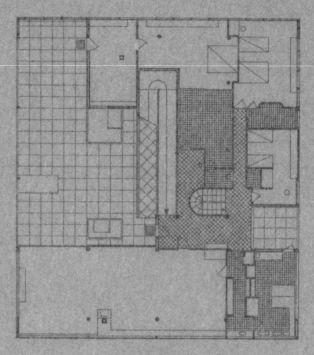

Villa Savoye at Poissy, 1929-1931.
Plan of the living quarters on the first floor, with terrace-roof.

Villa at Carthage, 1929.
Plan of the first floor.

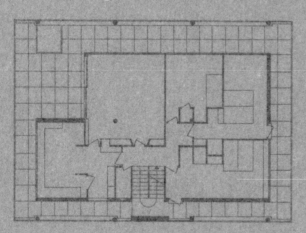

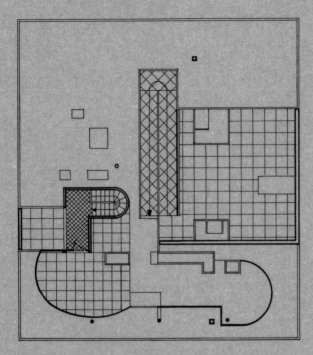

Villa Savoye at Poissy, 1929-1931.
Upper floor with sun patio.

Villa at Carthage, 1929.
Plan of the second floor.

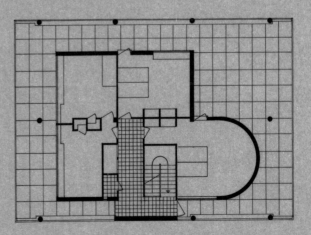

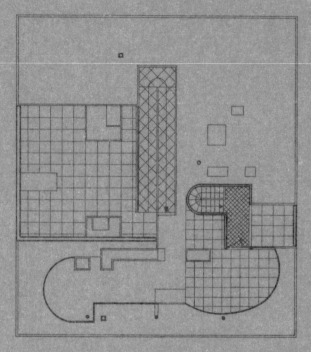

Villa Savoye at Poissy, 1929-1931.
Upper floor with sun patio.

Villa at Carthage, 1929.
Plan of the second floor.

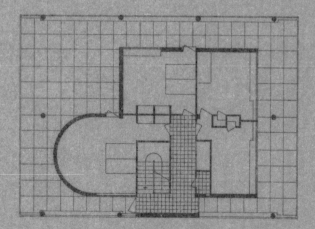

Villa Savoye at Poissy, bird's-eye view, 1929-1931.

Villa at Carthage, first project, 1928.

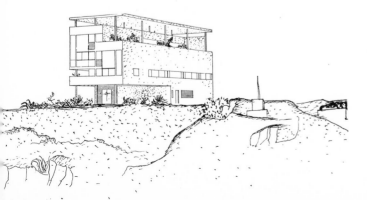

The terrace-roof is always presented by Le Corbusier as the natural complement of the free-standing supports (pilotis). Conceived as a sun patio or a roof garden in individual houses, it serves quite a different purpose in buildings of collective use—apartment blocks, like his Unités d'Habitation; office buildings, like the Secretariat at Chandigarh; or factories, like his industrial plant at Saint-Dié. Here it serves as a place where tenants, employees or workers can meet in leisure moments. It thus becomes, paradoxically, an essential element in the system of internal circulation, a "town-planning instrument," taking over an important share of the role played by the street and the square.

◀ *Apartment Block (Unité d'Habitation) at Marseilles, 1945-1952. Terrace-Roof.*

The Secretariat at Chandigarh, 1958. Terrace-Roof.

Villa at Garches, 1927.

the pillars were still included in the partitions, which were henceforth non-load-bearing and were produced in inexpensive materials. During the second stage, "the pillars left the corners and calmly stood in the middle of the rooms." Finally, "the chimneys left the walls." Research was directed towards a free redistribution of all the "organs" of the machine, with a view to improving their service-ability. As he developed the free plan to the full, "the stairways became free organs... Everywhere,

the organs took on an individual character, became free in relation to one another... The rooms, halls, other premises? They could henceforth be arranged at will, according to the most useful contingencies, on the basis of an independent organization." Two "organs," in particular, became detached from the walls, and more especially from the façades: the stairways (later, ramps) and the bathrooms; these were henceforth situated at the most convenient points and treated as independent plastic objects.

The free façade was a further consequence of the linear structural frame for, since the exterior walls were no longer load-bearing, they could be opened up or closed at will, in keeping with aesthetic or functional requirements. Taking advantage of this new freedom, Le Corbusier proceeded to replace the traditional window (a hole punched in the wall) by two new devices, the ribbon window and the glass wall. The ribbon window presented no particular problems, apart from aesthetic considerations; Perret, for example, always stood up for the window in the form of a glass door, higher than it is wide: "The window," he said, "is a man standing." The ribbon window first appeared in the La Roche and Jeanneret houses; in the next ten years it figured in nearly all Le Corbusier's projects, up to the rue Nungesser-et-Coli apartment house. As for the glass wall, it was a more delicate thing to handle. Forming large, empty, uniform surfaces,

Salvation Army Hostel in Paris, 1929-1933. Main Front (before it was altered).

Apartment Building in Geneva (Immeuble Clarté), 1930-1932. Detail of the North Front.

it ran the risk, under certain lighting conditions, of creating blank spaces incompatible with the unity and equilibrium of the overall design. And it might expose to view the life of the people inside. Above all, the glass wall was extremely sensitive to heat. He overcame these difficulties by inventing the sun-break (brise-soleil), a movable screen keeping the interior cool without obstructing the view out of doors,

breaking up the monotony of the glass wall, and at the same time ensuring privacy. Thus the "non-form" of the glass wall gave rise to a system of sun-control louvers extending over the entire façade, to the great visual enrichment of its design. The sun-break, like the pilotis, *has proved to be an architectural device rich in possibilities and admirably suited to modern buildings.*

Apartment House at 24, rue Nungesser-et-Coli, Paris, 1933.

In this methodical exploration of the free plan, economic considerations and plastic motivations joined with the determination to define a setting of everyday life in harmony with the "new spirit."

The same mechanical considerations which dictated the entire conception of the living-machine also suggested the principle of a new approach to space in three dimensions. "One day we noticed that the house, like the motor-car, could be a simple outer covering or membrane, containing multiple organs in free arrangement" (covering letter to the plan for a villa for Mme Meyer, 1925). Here, we are as far away from Perret and Frank Lloyd Wright, the two initiators of the free plan, as from the Russian Constructivists. The counterpoint which Le Corbusier here outlines between "membrane" and "organ" recalls neither the narrow rationalism of an Auguste Perret, whose ambitions scarcely went beyond "granting reinforced concrete its letters of nobility"; nor the archaic romanticism of a Wright, for whom the free expansion of the plan demonstrated the freedom of the individual, as master of the soil of which he had taken possession; nor yet the mechanical imitation of the Russians.

Frank Lloyd Wright, in the Larkin Building and Midway Gardens in Chicago and in several of his private houses, and Josef Hoffmann, in the Stoclet House in Brussels, had, even before the war, dealt skillfully with the introduction of different heights beneath the ceiling, and had made a large central space, with loggias opening on to it, the dominant feature of free architectural arrangements. For his part, Perret, at first in the rue Ponthieu garage and later, in still more spectacular fashion, in the Théâtre des Champs-Elysées, had used the concrete framework in analogous fashion, constructing different

levels freely in space. It was these examples that had inspired Le Corbusier in the Schwob House. But whereas, in the latter, as in the houses of Wright and of Hoffmann, the composition had remained predominantly horizontal, the twin-story mass merely contrasting with other single-story masses arranged around it, in the "living-machines" of the 1920's it was the twin-story residence, in which "the human animal could browse to his heart's content," that provided the true measure of the cell. Of the Villa Savoye, Le Corbusier said it was "not a composition of isolated cells, but a single mass divided in two by a floor": rooms and service premises, whose dimensions, following the example of sleeping-cars or liners, had been reduced to a rational minimum, were here introduced in the form of integrated "organs." In this way, the reinforced concrete framework made it possible for the free plan to incorporate the three dimensions of space.

This also made it possible to arrange freely the outer "membrane" in which the "organs" were placed: together with the free plan, it in fact provided the "free façade" as well. The latter, a surface of contact between interior mass and exterior space, a screen pierced with apertures for the passage of light, and liberated of all load-bearing function, could henceforth be treated exclusively in terms of its specific dual role of protective membrane and outer covering. The "organs" of which it was composed, walls and windows, could also be arranged quite freely; the window was now able to play the full part which accrued to it in the modulation of interior space through light. At the same time, the use of "regulating grids" made it possible to invest the pattern of the apertures with a dynamic equilibrium as rigorous as that of Mondrian's paintings.

View of the Weissenhof Settlement at Stuttgart, 1927. (Photograph taken shortly after its construction).

Early in 1927 Le Corbusier was invited by Mies van der Rohe, the architect in charge, to take part in the International Housing Exhibition in Stuttgart, sponsored by the Deutscher Werkbund. He accepted, and designed and built two houses in the experimental settlement constructed for the exhibition on the Weissenhof hill, overlooking Stuttgart.

This happened to be a particularly favorable time for a collective manifestation of modern architecture on the theme of house design and construction. In the draft program issued by the promoters of the exhibition (the local group of the Deutscher Werkbund), the main emphasis was laid on the problems of rationalization and standardization of building processes. Since 1918 several large-scale, industrialized building projects had been undertaken: in Holland first of all, where J.J.P. Oud was responsible for several

new housing estates in Rotterdam; then in Germany, both in Frankfort, where Ernst May carried out his famous suburban development of low-cost housing, and in Berlin, where Martin Wagner, City Architect from 1926, called on Mies, Gropius, Hugo Häring, Bruno Taut and other members of Der Ring, the Berlin architects' association, to carry out enormous housing projects. In France, too, in 1925, at Pessac near Bordeaux, Le Corbusier designed and built an advanced housing development, also making extensive use of mass-produced elements. The technical problems raised by large-scale housing schemes were thus being squarely faced by European architects. At the Weissenhof exhibition, however, Mies van der Rohe laid particular stress on the fact that, "be its technical and economic aspects ever so important, the problem of modern housing is, first

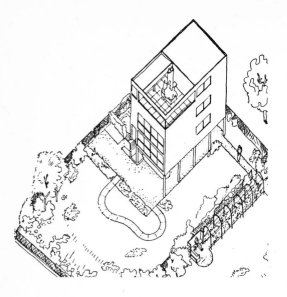

Le Corbusier: 2, Bruckmannweg.

Le Corbusier: 1-3, Rathenaustrasse.

and foremost, a problem of architecture. Rationalization and standardization are not the whole problem, they are a means which must on no account be taken as an end in itself. The problem of a new type of housing is a problem of the prevailing state of mind; the battle for new housing is only one aspect of the great fight for new forms of life."

Needless to say, this point of view was enthusiastically shared by the apostle of "the new spirit," and Le Corbusier leaped at the chance to take part in the Weissenhof exhibition. Among the other participants were Behrens, Poelzig, Gropius, Hilberseimer and Scharoun from Germany, Oud and Mart Stam from Holland, and Victor Bourgeois from Belgium. Conspicuous absentees were Erich Mendelsohn, Ernst May, Martin Wagner and Hugo Häring.

Mies van der Rohe drew up a remarkable site plan (partially carried out) and, for the rest, gave the participating architects complete freedom in their designs, with the one proviso that all the houses should have flat roofs. He himself built a small block of flats with a metal skeleton, in which he emphasized the flexibility of the plan. "Skeleton construction is the one best adapted to our needs. It enables us to rationalize the construction and to divide up the interior in complete freedom." This statement foreshadows the later work of Mies, and it is one that Le Corbusier would have been glad to endorse. Gropius declared that "the architect's main task today is that of an organizer who has to face up to all the biological, social, technical and plastic problems and synthesize them in an autonomous unity." At Weissenhof, he carried out a program which had been a long-standing preoccupation of his: the assemblying of isolated, prefabricated housing units. Oud, on the contrary, treated the case of housing units integrated into a continuous strip, in other words into an urban context, and designed them in terms of a classified system of internal and external circulation; for lack of space, however, this remarkable demonstration of the interdependence of architecture and town-planning could be only partially carried out. As for Le Corbusier, in the two houses he built for the Weissenhof exhibition, he provided the definitive formulation of his "Five Points."

The smaller of his two houses was the first actual example of the Citrohan unit he had designed in 1922. "An argument for modern housing is put forward here," he wrote. "A vast living room, in which one spends most of the day, in a well-being ensured by large dimensions and plenty of air and light; giving on to this room are smaller premises adapted to functions of short duration, functions for which the room-size required by the building regulations is too big..." This house was designed so that further units could be added to it at will, either beside it or on top of it. The other, larger house, comprising two apartments, illustrated "the same argument, but in a different form": "The main room is obtained by the eclipse of the movable partitions, which are used only at night in order to make the house into a kind of sleeping-car... A small side corridor, of exactly the same size as those in sleeping-cars..." The use of prefabricated parts in this "living-machine" was carried very far.

The Weissenhof exhibition attracted a great deal of attention, and it demonstrated the unity of purpose and idiom prevailing among the most progressive European architects. Le Corbusier, in France, declared that "there is nothing to be ashamed of in having a house that is as practical as a typewriter." Hilberseimer, in Germany, agreed with him: "The best home will be the one that is treated like a perfect object of use." So did Mart Stam in Holland: "To any clear and honest mind, the home is an object of use." The rejection of display and the insistence on honesty were common to all, and so was the use of a formal idiom essentially Purist or Neo-Plasticist: the terrace-roof was an article of faith in their credo. In June 1928, less than a year after the Weissenhof exhibition, Le Corbusier and other leading architects met at the Château de La Sarraz in Switzerland to form the CIAM (Congrès Internationaux d'Architecture Moderne). The theme of their first congress, held at Frankfort in 1929, was the very one which the Stuttgart exhibition had shown to be the main concern of progressive architects: low-cost housing. So in this respect the Weissenhof confrontation was a signal success: it brought the most progressive architects together and gave them a sense of solidarity. On the other hand, it also gave rise to the first great newspaper campaign against modern architecture, and it attracted the attention of Nazi agitators who now began their campaign against "degenerate architecture" and "boulevard architecture," of which Le Corbusier, from this time on, was made the scapegoat—"the Trojan horse of Bolshevism," as he was called.

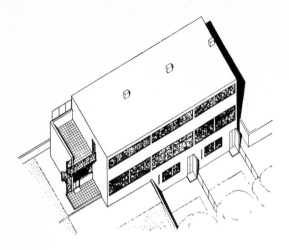

Mart Stam (1899): 24-28, Am Weissenhof.

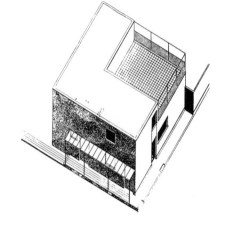

Hans Scharoun (1893): 1, Hölzelweg.

Walter Gropius (1883): 4, Bruckmannweg. (This house was subsequently altered)

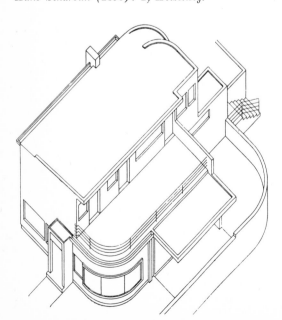

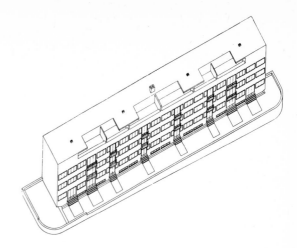

Ludwig Mies van der Rohe (1886):
14-20, Am Weissenhof.

J.J.P. Oud (1890-1963): 1-9, Pankokweg.

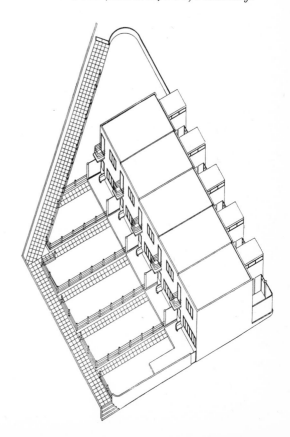

Merely to list the five basic points of the new architecture—"free-standing supports *(pilotis)*, free plan, terrace-roof, free façade, ribbon window"— might leave the impression that Le Corbusier had done no more than combine and develop in systematic fashion certain concepts encountered in haphazard fashion among his forerunners. Did not the *pilotis* derive directly from Perret's concrete framework? Do we not find the free plan in the work of Frank Lloyd Wright long before the First World War? the free façade in Adolf Loos? the terrace-roof in Tony Garnier? and the ribbon window in Loos and the Dutch school? As for the twin-story residence with loggias: had this not been a current feature in Paris, in artists' studios, since the Second Empire? Yet it is obvious that Le Corbusier produced something far more than the mere sum or synthesis of these concepts. Each one of them was thought out afresh in terms of an "organ" in a machine that was conceived of from the first as constituting a unit from both functional and spatial points of view. In place of the additive method, which proceeded by more or less free composition of masses largely determined by structural limitations, Le Corbusier introduced a diametrically opposite approach, which recognized only an outer covering independent of the ground and containing free organs, limited solely by organizational and plastic requirements.

To conceive of a building in this way—no longer in terms of composition but in terms of an organism or a machine—amounted to breaking with all conventions, to introducing into architectural thought ideas that were not only novel but even scandalous: for instance, concepts of weightlessness and mobility. There appeared, moreover, to be some inherent contradiction in the equilibrium which Le Corbusier claimed to establish between the expansion of organs freely creating their own space and the strict limitations of the spatial unit determined by the outer covering. No less disturbing was his reinterpretation of the whole concept of plan, a reinterpretation to which he attached a primordial importance.

It is in a brief phrase in *Vers une architecture* that we find the key to this problem: "The eye of the spectator moves over a site..." and, in moving, sees architecture born. In other words, the plan is not an abstract factor, but the organizational scheme of a visual experience which takes place in movement and unfolds in time—the scenario of an "architectural promenade." Writing of the La Roche House, Le Corbusier said: "One enters. The architectural spectacle presents itself successively to the eye. The spectator follows an itinerary and the scenes unfold in a wide variety of forms. There is the play of inflowing light illuminating the walls or creating half-lights. The bays provide views of the exterior, where (thanks to the right-angle arrangement of the house and the indentations formed by the outer covering) one discovers architectural unity once more."

Thus, movement first and then, at once, light, which is reflected by the walls or absorbed by the hollows modulating the space. Of the Green Mosque at Brussa (Turkey), Le Corbusier once said that conceiving such a plan was equivalent to "subjecting the visitor to a sensorial rhythm, conceiving a motive purpose" which gave birth to "a world in itself." Light and movement were the means by which the building "said what it had to say."

"One works with walls, straight or curved, a stretch of ground, apertures for the passage of men or of light, doors or windows; the apertures lighten or darken, gladden or sadden, the walls are bursting with light or reposing in half-light, or in shadow, rendering gay, serene, or sad; your symphony is all set." Because he regarded the wall, not as an obstacle to light but as a reflector of light, Le Corbusier was able to write (in *Vers une architecture*) this at first sight singular phrase: "Have respect for the wall. The men of Pompeii did not pierce their walls; they *paid homage to the wall, they had a love of light*." Color extends, at times even amends, the effect of light: "The first experiments in multicolor (in the La Roche House), based on the specific reactions of the colors, introduced the possibility of architectural camouflage, i.e. the emphasizing of certain masses or, alternatively, their effacement." Multicolor, however, was only justified by the presence of white; color must never be allowed to confuse shapes or situations: "the interior of the house must be white but, for the white to be appreciated, a carefully devised multicolor scheme is also necessary." The principle was always to "consider color as a contributor of space."

This dynamic, rhythmic interpretation of the free plan, this use of color, no longer for decorative but constructive ends, displays evident affinities with other experiments of the time. True, the primacy which Le Corbusier accorded to light, or more precisely to the play of light reflected upon smooth surfaces, is alone sufficient to set him very far apart from Frank Lloyd Wright. At the same time, his constant desire, on the one hand, to ensure a flexible sequence of spatial situations, on the other, to eliminate masses in order to amplify the development of space—these are features to be found in varying degrees among all the representatives of the modern movement of the 1920's. Even so, there was not one of them in whom they aroused a lyricism of compar-

able intensity, unless it be Mies van der Rohe. As for multicolor as an architectural device, this had been studied by De Stijl ever since 1917.

Le Corbusier had doubtless known of the Dutch experiments of van Doesburg, perhaps since 1920, at the latest since 1923, the date of the exhibition of projects in Neo-Plasticist architecture at the Galerie Rosenberg in Paris. Nevertheless, while it is true that the crystallization of observations made since the journey to the East in 1910 was largely due to the example of De Stijl, it is no less certain that the multicolor technique of the La Roche and Pessac houses drew its inspiration from the specific experiment of Purism. Not only did it retain the muted chromatism of the latter, but also the determination to preserve the density, the physical reality, of the elements of the composition. It was this determination which led Le Corbusier to reject abstraction.

The contrast established, from the very first of these Purist houses, between plane or concave screens articulating freely with one another and highly individualized plastic objects is what distinguishes the architectural space of Le Corbusier most clearly from that of Mies van der Rohe. In the latter's German Pavilion in Barcelona, for instance, only the free surfaces intervene in order to mark the essential stages in the unfolding of the "architectural promenade," which is even more fluid, though less animated, less rich in inventions and surprises, than at the Villa Savoye. Moreover, in the case of Mies, this "promenade" is developed on one level only and does not lead to that complete take-over of space in three dimensions which characterizes all of Le Corbusier's projects.

Yet, however original Le Corbusier's plastic expression and "motive purpose" may be, it is of less importance for our understanding of his work than his tenacious, impassioned determination to discipline this wealth, to classify clearly and simply the "architectural events" which occur at every stage of the promenade, to envelop the complexity of it in a "unity" which would transform the house—itself a simple architectural event situated in an always infinitely complex site ("the outside is always an inside")—into an element of order and serenity. In the letter to Mme Meyer already cited, Le Corbusier gave powerful expression to this classical will for unity: "We dreamed of making you a house which would be smooth and plain like a well-proportioned chest and which would not be marred by multiple accidents which create a picturesque element that is both artificial and illusory, which do not ring true beneath the light, and which only add to the surrounding tumult... Do not imagine that the smoothness is the result of idleness; on the contrary, it is the outcome of long-matured plans, the simple is not easy... To tell the truth, it is there that the greatest difficulty in architecture lies: in getting things back into line once more." But: "We believe that unity is more powerful than the parts." The famous drawing of the four compositions and the lapidary commentary accompanying it retraced the highlights in this struggle for the mastery of unity. For Le Corbusier, the house, an individual cell for living in, must always remain potentially capable of combination; it must be capable of being integrated within a more complex grouping, inside which it would find itself on a footing of equality with others. In this sense, too, the "living-machine" remained an "article of mass production."

Above:
La Roche House, Paris, 1923. Hall (present state).

Below:
La Roche House, Paris, 1923. Hall
(shortly after being built).

◄ *The entrance hall is a room with triple floor height and no ceiling. From here, access is had by both stairs and ramps to the living areas of the house (dining room and bedroom, upper photo) and the reception area (drawing room and library, lower photo). The hall serves not only to connect these two zones but to set them distinctly apart.*

"We'll get the painters in to blow up the walls that stand ►
in our way," wrote Le Corbusier. "Architectural polychromy seizes the entire wall and qualifies it with the powerful throb of the blood, or the freshness of the prairie, or the glow of the sun, or the depth of sea and sky. Think of the forces available! This is dynamics, or I might just as well say dynamite, having let my painter into the house. If this or that wall is blue, it recedes; if it is red, it holds the plane, or brown; I can paint it black, or yellow... Architectural polychromy doesn't kill the walls, but it can move them back and classify them in order of importance. Here a skillful architect has wholesome and powerful resources to draw on. Polychromy belongs to the great living architecture of all times and of tomorrow. Wall-paper has enabled us to see the matter clearly, to repudiate deceitful trick effects and open all doors to great bursts of color, dispenser of space and classifier of essential things and accessory things. Color is as powerful an instrument of architecture as the plan and the section are. Better still: color is the very element of the plan and the section."

On the use of polychromy inside the house, Le Corbusier, in a conversation with Fernand Léger, declared himself in full agreement with Dutch architects, while paying tribute to Léger as a pioneer in this line of research (in which he himself was also a pioneer). On the other hand, he reproached the Dutch for using polychromy on the outside of the house; there, he said, "it destroys, dislocates, divides, and so works against unity." When in 1925 he too resorted to external polychromy in order to organize the volumes of his houses at Pessac, he did so in a wholly different spirit, which he defined as follows: "There emerges from the Pessac houses

Theo van Doesburg (1883-1931)
and Cornelis van Eesteren (1897):
Architectural Project, 1923.

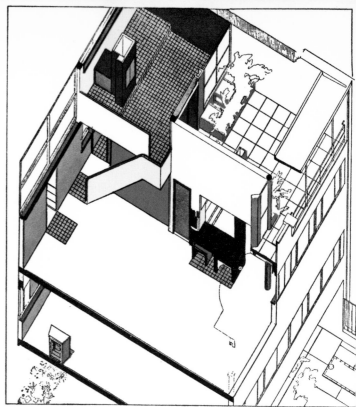

Cook House at Boulogne-sur-Seine, 1926.

a new, unexpected aesthetic. But this aesthetic is legitimate, conditioned, on the one hand, by the imperatives of the construction and on the other by the primordial basis of architectural sensation—volume. The houses, standing beside each other, comply with rules of proportion, they are governed by relationships which we have tried to render eloquent and harmonious. We have also applied an entirely new conception of polychromy, with a distinctly architectural aim in view: to model space by means of the physical properties of color, to emphasize certain masses in the housing development, and to tone down certain others—in a word, to compose with color as we did with forms. To do this was to lead architecture into town-planning."

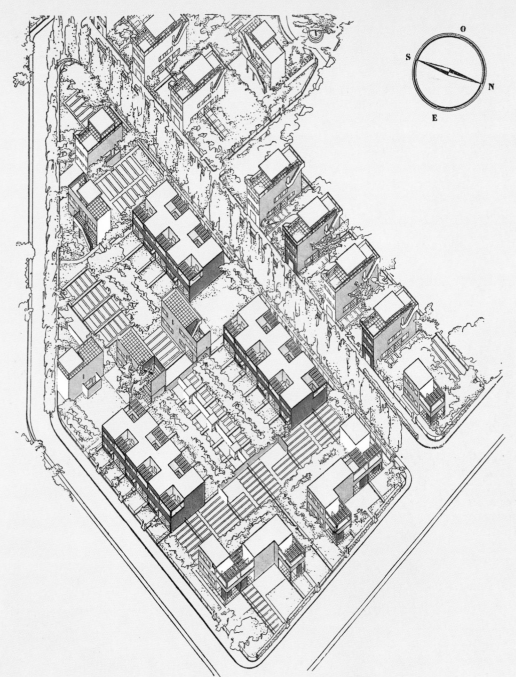

Plan of the Housing Development at Pessac, near Bordeaux, 1925.

The Four Compositions:

1. La Roche-Jeanneret Houses in Paris, 1923.
2. Villa at Garches, 1927.
3. Villa at Carthage, 1929.
4. Villa Savoye at Poissy, 1929-1931.

"A building is like a soap bubble. The bubble is perfectly harmonious if the breath is evenly applied, evenly regulated from the inside. The outside is the result of an inside." Le Corbusier himself often referred back to his famous drawing of the "four compositions," in which he summed up the "aesthetic alarums" he went through before he arrived at that "harmonious application of the breath" which sets the building in perfect equilibrium with its environment and makes of the envelope a membrane clearly separating the two things, while promoting with maximum efficiency the osmosis between them. When he wrote that "the outside is the result of an inside," he meant that the envelope expresses the organization of the volumes; but these volumes may just as well be external as internal. Compositions 1 and 2 fix the limits of the possible relations between the enclosed volumes and the surrounding space, while 3 and 4 represent two successive attempts to maintain the unity of the design while opening it up as fully as possible (see p. 99 for the plans). It is interesting to compare these last two houses with the Neo-Plasticist villa designed by Mies van der Rohe for the Weissenhof exhibition (p. 89).

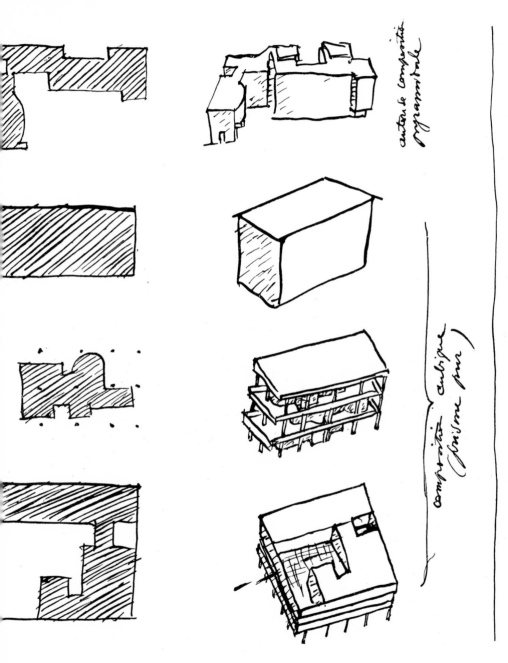

genre plutôt facile,
pittoresque
mouvementé
On peut toutefois le
discipliner par classement
et hiérarchie

autour de composité
pyramidale

très difficile
(satisfaction de l'esprit)

très facile,
pratique
combinable

composité cubique
(prisme pur)

très généreux
on affirme à l'extérieur
une volonté architecturale,
on satisfait à l'intérieur
à tous les besoins fonctionnels
(insolation, contiguïtés,
circulation.

Swiss Pavilion at the Cité Universitaire, Paris, 1930-1932. South Front.

For Le Corbusier, the "architectural promenade" was not an episodic delight reserved for the aesthete or the specialist; it had nothing to do with recreation or picturesqueness. It was the very substance of the architectural experience: "Forms in light. *Inside, and outside; below, and above. Inside: you enter, you walk about and look around you, and the forms explain themselves, they develop, they combine. Outside: you approach, you see, you get interested, you* appreciate, you go all the way around, you discover things. You keep getting different impressions, one after the other. And the game being played becomes apparent. You walk about, you keep moving and turning around. Note what sort of apparatus man responds to architecture with: he has two eyes which can only look ahead; he can turn his head sideways or upwards, he can turn his body, or carry his body along on his legs and keep turning all the while. It takes* *hundreds of successive perceptions to make up his architectural sensation. It is his promenade, his ramble, that counts, that is the prime mover of architectural events. Therefore the game being played has not been set out around a fixed, central, ideal, rotary point, a point of simultaneous circular vision. That is the architecture of the Schools, the academies, the decadent fruit of the Great Renaissance, the death of architecture, its petrification."*

The Villa Savoye concludes the series of "promenades" opened by the La Roche house. It realizes the ambitious project of integrating the internal space and an extended external space into the dimensions of the "four horizons":
"The site: a vast lawn bulging out like a flattened dome. The main view is to the north, which means away from the sun; so the normal front of the house would be in the wrong direction. The house is a box in the air, pierced all around, uninterruptedly, with a window extending lengthwise.

Villa Savoye at Poissy, 1929-1931. North Corner.

East Corner.

South Corner.

West Corner.

No more hesitation about making architectural play with the solid and hollow parts of the building. The box stands amid the meadows, overlooking the orchard. Under the box, between the free-standing supports, runs a driveway. Cars can come and go by means of a hairpin turn, whose curve encloses, right under the supports, the entrance of the house, the hall, the garage and the service premises (laundry, linen room, servants' quarters).

"From the hall, a gently sloping ramp leads up almost imperceptibly to the first floor, where the living areas are: drawing room, bedrooms, etc. Looking out on the view and the light from the regular sides of the box, the different rooms stand elbow to elbow around a garden that acts as a distributor of proper light and sun.

"Opening on the hanging garden in complete freedom are the sliding walls of plate glass of the drawing room and several other rooms of the house: so the sun streams in everywhere, into the very heart of the house.

"From the hanging garden, the ramp, external now, leads up to the roof, to the solarium.

"The latter, moreover, is connected by the three flights of a spiral staircase with the cellar dug in the ground under the free-standing supports. This spiral, a pure vertical organ, fits freely into the horizontal composition.

"To conclude, look at the section: air circulates everywhere, there is light at all points, it reaches everywhere. A walk through the house produces architectural impressions of a diversity that disconcerts every visitor unaware of the architectural liberties made possible by modern techniques. The simple stilts of the ground floor are so arranged as to pattern the landscape with a regularity whose effect is to do away with any notion of a 'front' or 'back' or 'side' of the house.

"The plan is a pure one, made to answer as closely as possible to actual needs. And in the rural landscape of Poissy, it is in the right place.

"You will not mind, I hope, my having developed before your eyes this example of liberties taken. They have been taken because they have been won, torn from the quickening sources of modern material. Poetry and lyricism brought forth by technics."

Ramp and Staircase leading to the first floor living quarters.

Ramp leading to the Sun Patio.

Terrace-Roof.

Poissy is less than an hour's drive from Paris,
in the Seine valley. The site of the Villa Savoye
is now ruined and it requires an effort to imagine
the harmony that originally prevailed between
the natural setting and the life of the people who
lived here. But under the changing sky there
remains—and nothing can destroy this—an
extraordinary movement of musically vibrant
space. Standing vacant, having ceased to function
as a "living-machine," the villa, with its geometric
silhouette, rises up before the passer-by like a
creation of the mind—reminiscent in this respect
of the geometric buildings designed in the
eighteenth century by another rationalist visionary, Claude-Nicolas Ledoux, for his "ideal city"
of Chaux.

Space and Plasticity

I compose with light.

Lobby of the Assembly Hall at Chandigarh (Punjab), 1961.

JUST as Le Corbusier's Purist sketches of bottles and glasses are nowadays classified with those experiments which, on the morrow of the First World War, ended up by overcoming the contradictions of Cubism, so, too, the "living-machines" which he planned or built between 1922 and 1930 have long been consigned to the imaginary museum of machine civilization, together with the Delages and the Voisins of their owners, Tatlin's tower, the Bauhaus, the Total Theater and the *Ballet mécanique*, the glass skyscrapers of Mies, the "Prouns" of Lissitzky, and Gabo's plexiglass. They have their place there alongside those constructions, long since cast aside, which at one time embodied the optimistic hopes of that "white world" of blissful certainties, of which van Doesburg declared, in 1927, that it would wipe out the very memory of the "brown world" of sentimental pusillanimity and decorative ambiguity.

It is both tempting and facile, but ultimately somewhat vain, to contrast the lightness and reserve of these houses with the plastic density and "brutalism" of those vast buildings which Le Corbusier,

◄ *View of Le Corbusier's Studio at 24, rue Nungesser-et-Coli, Paris, showing the rubblework of the back wall, 1933. (Photo taken during the artist's lifetime).*

after fifteen years of almost total architectural inactivity, produced between 1950 and 1965. Who was Le Corbusier the architect? The austere engineer of Purism, the classicist paradoxically bent on "forcing back into line" the very forms that he had but recently liberated? Or the impassioned plastic artist who, in his sixties, was to develop them with an insistence sometimes described, to his annoyance, as Baroque; who juggled with masses in a manner admittedly spectacular, but in which one can detect the very negation of that mobility, that dematerialization of the architectural envelope of space to which he had acceded twenty-five years earlier?

The answer to this question is not likely to be found by contrasting the two formal idioms, purist and lyrical, in which Le Corbusier is alleged successively to have expressed himself; still less by opposing these two idioms in rhetorical fashion. For though Le Corbusier, more than any other protagonist of twentieth-century architecture, had the redoubtable gift of transmuting in forms (and forms couched in violently personal tones) all his spatial intuitions and all the functional relations he intended to establish, he never in fact directed his researches towards the creation of forms, still less towards the elaboration of a "style." The bold plastic invention of his

Once he had gone beyond the white abstraction of his Purist houses, the texture of the building materials became a more and more conspicuous feature of Le Corbusier's architecture. Though he never toned them down, but on the contrary made a point of laying stress on contrasting masses and textures, the materials he used were few in number. The craftsmanlike preciosity and the taste for patiently elaborated textural effects that one finds in Perret or Mies are as foreign to him as the surface effects so widely used in contemporary architecture. Le Corbusier treats his materials no differently than he does architectural polychromy: to him they are a means of structuring space. Thus his contrasts are concerned with fundamental qualities: rough or smooth, dull or luminous textures, heavy or fluid, transparent or opaque, broken or continuous masses.

◀ Swiss Pavilion at the Cité Universitaire, Paris, 1930-1932. Smooth stone-veneer finish of the building and rubblestone wall below.

Brazilian Pavilion at the Cité Universitaire, Paris, ▶ 1957-1959.
Imprint of the formwork left visible on the concrete according to Le Corbusier's instructions.

architecture is doubtless unique, doubtless fascinating, and we have him to thank for some of the most powerful emotions engendered by the builder's art for many, many years. But it is equally obvious that this invention has been the cause of serious misunderstandings. It is over and beyond this "play of forms in light"—which some regarded as "masterly, correct, and magnificent," but others as sterile and rhetorical—that we shall find the elements we need in order to identify, and perhaps even to judge, Le Corbusier the architect.

Moreover, though the renewal of the plastic idiom appeared (in Marseilles) in a manner that surprised the broad public, it had in fact been initiated many years previously. It is enough to recall the numerous projects (and rare constructions) of the period preceding the Second World War to show that, from 1930 onwards, Le Corbusier gradually abandoned that Purist transparency which in fact he had already discarded in his painting as early as 1927-1928. In the Swiss Pavilion, for instance, the *pilotis* are sculpted in the mass and a panel of millstone grit somewhat incongruously breaks up the unity of the smooth surfaces. The skyscraper planned for Algiers is encased in sun-breaks of deep-shadowed egg-crate pattern. The forms become denser, archaic constructional motifs appear (e.g. the flat vaults of La Celle-Saint-Cloud). Concrete, hitherto concealed or enclosed in a smooth white wash, is henceforth displayed with increasing vigor as a material in its own right, with its burrs and its greyness; rubblestone, as used in the Mathes and Pradot villas, even penetrates as

◀ *Church of Ronchamp, near Belfort, 1950-1953.*
West wall with white plastering and tank
of rough concrete under the roof spout.

far as the studio of the rue Nungesser-et-Coli, where Le Corbusier, in a type of architectural *collage* without precedent, preserved as such the dividing wall joined by masonry to the next-door house. Then came the adoption of coarse wood (as in the Errazuris house in Chile) and bare brick—poor man's materials, but weighty, granular, veined, and rough, making their presence felt at once by their texture and their mass.

The year 1930 marked the beginnings of the break-up of the rigid, abstract unity of Purist expression, at the very time when the movement known as international architecture was entering upon a crisis. This crisis was brought on not only by external events—the economic depression, the brutal suppression of the German movement, at once so vital and so vitalizing—but also by certain aesthetic factors of profound significance. At that time, in Europe at least, secondary techniques, in particular the climatization and protection of exterior surfaces, had not yet reached a stage which made it possible to effect that almost total dematerialization of the envelope called for by the advances achieved in construction proper, and which the post-Cubist aesthetic demanded. The failure of the "exact glass wall" *(pan de verre exacte)*, the poor quality of the wall-coatings, the limitations of country building-yards (Pradot, Mathes), all these factors induced Le Corbusier to temper his intransigence as regards materials. Then came the years of penury, during which Le Corbusier, with nothing on his order books and virtually without resources in a Europe bled white by war, was to suffer great hardship. Not so Gropius and Mies, who, emigrating, after a few difficult years, to a land where the economy was thriving and technology highly developed, never had occasion to cultivate the sense of poverty to the same degree.

Yet, even though it did not come suddenly, did not the revival of the architectural idiom signify the rejection of the mobility, the weightlessness, and so, ultimately, of that freedom of space, the conquest of which the Purist houses had so triumphantly sung? Was it not a type of camouflage behind which the ageing Le Corbusier—aware that the absence of all chance of experimentation between the ages of forty-five and sixty had left him rooted to theoretical positions now outmoded—endeavored to conceal from himself this period of experimental stagnation by giving free vent to the whims of his imagination? The "free plan," the "free façade," did not these become pretexts for exercises in purely formal virtuosity, indulged in by a more and more insatiable passion for plastic expression? Or was there not—parallel with the exploration of new possibilities of expression through form and matter—a continuation and development of that concept of plan, of "motive purpose," in which Le Corbusier had detected, ever since 1921, the dynamic generator of all architecture? And, with the metamorphosis of the envelope—no longer "smooth and plain like a well-proportioned chest," but itself an increasingly complex plastic reality—a radical revision in the relationship between inside space and outside space?

The 1931 project for a Museum of Modern Art, subsequently taken up several times, coincides in time with the completion of the Villa Savoye. It is of interest to us not so much for the manner in which the specific program of the museum is treated (singularly novel though that was) as for the spatial proposals, of much more general application, that it contains. From the principle of the distinction, introduced with the *pilotis*, between two superimposed and independent zones, one reserved for traffic and the other for accommodation, Le Corbusier deduced a further principle: that of continuous structures, suspended above the ground and developing freely in the horizontal plane. In 1925, almost simultaneously with the *immeuble-villas* in which the cells were grouped vertically, Le Corbusier had drawn up a project for a Cité Universitaire, in which he proposed a horizontal arrangement—webbed and virtually without façade, i.e. with no envelope—of individual cells in juxtaposition along the ground. The project made full use of the terrace-roof as a "bringer of light," introducing skylights and saw-tooth roofs to illuminate the masses enclosed in a compact structure. But this project did not solve the problem of internal and external traffic. In the Museum, by contrast, and under the Museum, the traffic problem was solved with what was in theory complete freedom: not only did the ground level remain reserved for external traffic, but the system of access via the center (already used in the Villa Savoye) made it possible to develop the "motive purpose" of the interior circuit through the full circle of 360 degrees, instead of 180, as hitherto. The square spiral on which this circuit was articulated invests a cellular structure (the project is conceived in terms of an integral prefabricated unit) with a mobility that is no longer merely virtual, optical—as it was with the "boxes on stilts" which aroused the wrath of Frank Lloyd Wright—but is real, and allows the structure literally to progress, creating a form of architecture that moves and is capable of transformation. The theme of the variability and mobility of the constructed mass had hitherto been examined (notably in the Bauhaus) only in relation to the individual house, and always, incidentally, in connection with research on prefabrication. In the

Museum of Unlimited Growth, Le Corbusier developed it for the first time on a far wider scale, a scale which was still that of architecture, but was potentially that of town-planning: capable of modification at all times and in all places (by removal or suppression of floor, wall, or roof), the Museum is the first example of an architectural structure conceived of as a method of organizing space, and no longer as a mere form expressing a given aesthetic canon.

Neither the Cité Universitaire nor the Musée à Croissance Illimitée were to be realized (the museums in Tokyo and in Ahmedabad are only fragmentarily derived from the 1931 idea), but the very method which had inspired this idea was to lead Le Corbusier, shortly before his death, to propose, within the framework of a totally different program, a solution which seemed surprising only in the light of his recent plastic accomplishments in Ronchamp and in Chandigarh (Punjab). In his project for a hospital in Venice, Le Corbusier in fact combined the grouping in horizontal units of cells illuminated from above (which was the basis of the University City of 1925) with the principle of structuration of space in superimposed layers and a system of internal and external traffic narrowly overlapping yet independent, based on central access (which formed the essential elements of the plan for the Museum of Unlimited Growth). A piece of continuous, suspended architecture, the façade-less hospital in Venice did not grow, like the Museum, through a series of concentric spirals, but rather through the juxtaposition of blocks, corresponding to the different wards, distributed over a grid sufficiently flexible to ensure its integration within the most closely-knit urban network. As in the University City, the cells (patients' rooms), concentrated in the upper stories, were illuminated

Ahmedabad Museum (Punjab), 1956-1957.

Museum of Modern Western Art, Tokyo, 1957-1959.

from above. The "reversal of the plan" thus led not only to an inversion of the pyramid formed by each unit, which rested on the ground on its apex, but to the actual suppression of the envelope. While the effect of weightlessness was not expressed in such directly recognizable form as in the Weissenhof or the Villa Savoye, the principle was nonetheless retained, and new conclusions drawn therefrom, the objective at all times being a more complete and flexible mastery over the three dimensions of space.

The project for the Museum of Unlimited Growth is important for a proper understanding of the direction of Le Corbusier's researches not only because of the clear-cut manner in which the principle of continuous and variable structures emerges from that of suspended architecture. The project also represents an extreme example of treating the plan in terms of movements by the spectator, i.e. in terms of motion. The intuition which enabled Le Corbusier to abolish the classic concept of the room and to treat the museum as a veritable thoroughfare, interspersed with "encounters" representing so many "events" for stimulating "meditation," could only derive from a way of thinking completely dominated by the idea of circulation, i.e. of intercourse and exchange within the architectural organism. Such a preoccupation found expression, at the town-planning level, in the search for continuity and classification of traffic ways. In the field of architecture itself, however, it was the solution accorded to the traffic problem which provided the key to each project.

In the case of large public buildings, the architect was faced with the problem of disposal and outlet for very considerable masses of people. The solutions devised, and always renewed, are at times breathtaking, as in the Palace of the Soviets or, thirty years later, the church at Firminy. As for the Assembly Hall at Chandigarh, it called for a subtle hierarchical differentiation between the various circuits (ministers, M.P.'s, visitors, employees, etc.). The network which Le Corbusier evolved here heralded the even more complex web of independent circuits in the Venice hospital.

In the projects for the secondary and tertiary sectors, the access to places of work—the internal traffic of personnel and of goods—gave rise to experiments whose interest extends well beyond the plane of simple organizational techniques (Rentenanstalt, Green Factory, Olivetti Electronic Center). In the multicellular schemes for collective housing, the problem of internal traffic ways arises in still more acute form: it is they which in fact determine the relations between neighbors, the relations of the cell with its "extensions," the relations of the individual and the community. It was at La Tourette that Le Corbusier gave the most extreme expression to the differentiation of "conduits" classed according to their function in the life of the community: corridors serving the cells, halls for meetings, the processional pathway giving access to the church, or the promenade for solitary meditation on the roof. But it was also on the basis of the articulation of traffic ways that he defined the apartment block: interior streets concealed from view, rapid vertical drainage, and, on the roof, the piazza for promoting human contacts and serving for collective pursuits.

Project for the Palace of the Soviets in Moscow, 1931. Model (above), sketches (left) and plan (right). ▶

The different buildings are linked together by a unity of design similar to that which had impressed Le Corbusier in the arrangement of the baptistery, cathedral and leaning tower at Pisa (as seen in his sketch, below left).

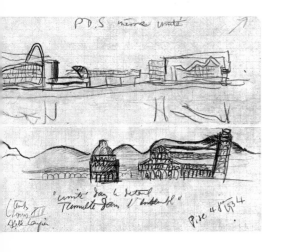

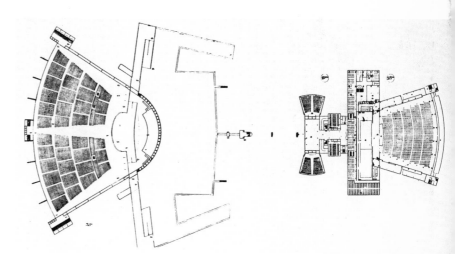

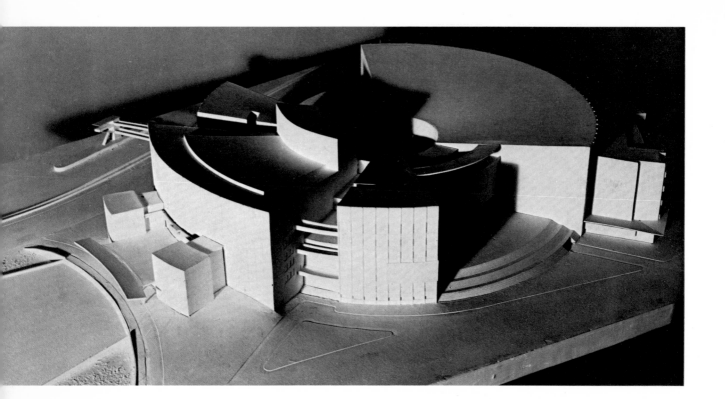

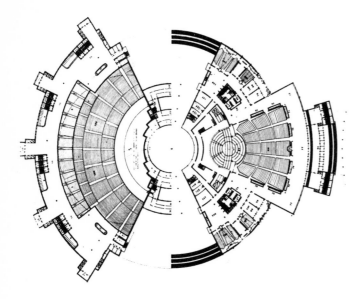

Walter Gropius (1883).
Model and Plan for the Palace of the Soviets.

Page 119: Naum Gabo (1890).
Sketch and Plan for the Palace of the Soviets.

Page 120: Erich Mendelsohn (1887-1953).
Model and Plan for the Palace of the Soviets.

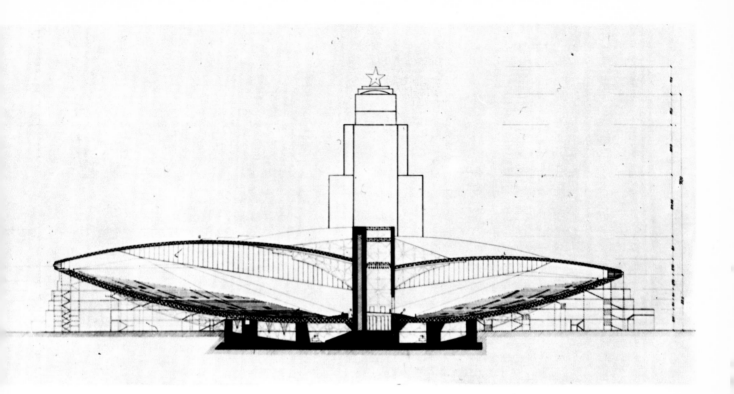

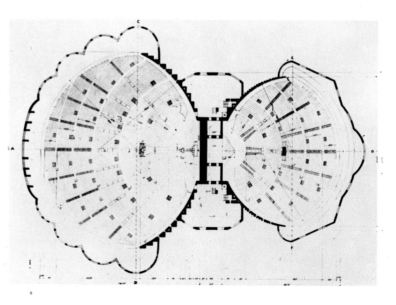

From his constant endeavor to safeguard the exact interplay of interior and exterior relations which characterized each building, Le Corbusier evolved a plastic idiom of movement apparently inexhaustible in its wealth: "conduits" (La Tourette, Chandigarh), stairways (La Roche house, Swiss Pavilion, rue Nungesser-et-Coli, Marseilles), interior ramps (Villa Savoye, Chandigarh), exterior ramps (Harvard, Ahmedabad, Strasbourg)—all of these were used to punctuate all the "architectural promenades" to which his imagination gave birth.

The novelty of this idiom gave rise, among countless imitators, to a veritable rhetoric not of movement but of restlessness. But since these forms, unlike those of Le Corbusier, did not derive from a genuine intuition of the mobility of space, but remained independent plastic entities assembled from outside, they usually produce an impression of heaviness and verbosity; moreover, they were to be the cause of a long-standing misconception concerning the sense of Le Corbusier's architectural research after 1950, which was in fact a search for the mobility and flexibility of spatial development, not for the monumental assertion of the isolated form.

While the project for the Museum of Unlimited Growth derived from the extrapolation of the open-plan concept, as realized in the "living-machines," it yet seemed to put an end once and for all to that search for the unity of the outer covering "smooth and plain like a well-proportioned chest," within which Le Corbusier had hitherto tried to contain the expansion of this plan. As an elementary spatial unit, virtually capable of multiplication, the living-machine must submit to the law of standardization and "get back into line."

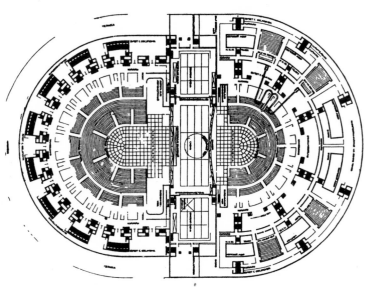

The idea of building a Palace of the Soviets was mooted in Russia as soon as the Revolution took place. An initial visionary approach to the scheme was Tatlin's projected Tower of 1919, which was to rise to a height of nearly 2000 feet and be partially movable around a slanting axis; but it was technically and economically unrealizable at that time. Shelved, then taken up again from time to time, the Palace project was widely publicized in 1931 when the Soviet government announced an international competition for it, open to architects all over the world. The competition aroused considerable interest among designers of all tendencies and gave rise to an exciting confrontation of ideas. In the end, the prize was awarded to a mediocre project submitted by an academic group of Russian architects.

The competitors, ranging from Perret to Gabo, from Poelzig to Ginzburg, naturally approached the problem from many different points of view. Some of the projects however, indeed the most significant among them, show in their general design certain similarities well enough marked for it to be possible to define with some precision the differences in outlook behind these projects—those, notably, of Gropius, Mendelsohn, Le Corbusier and Gabo (the latter's designs were not officially submitted and never went beyond the stage of sketches).

These four projects have in common the arrangement of the two large assembly halls, standing front to front. Each of these halls took the form of a segment of a circle, within the circumference of which the plan as a whole was roughly enclosed. It was the project of Gropius that approximated most closely to this ideal form, a form which, in combination with the square and the triangle, was fundamental to the Bauhaus approach to the teaching of design and technics; yet the virtuosity with which Gropius fitted together the different elements of his plan is quite in the classical tradition. Erich Mendelsohn, on the other hand, worked outwards from a stated volume and crowned the whole building with an enormous hemispherical dome, in which he inserted a prism placed on a slab running at right angles to the axis on which the two halls are aligned. He evidently relied on optical distortions to give this composite volume that "infinite dimension" on which he had laid so much stress in his war-time designs. Gabo too resorted to shell structures, but he turned them over like basins which he disposed symmetrically on either side of a signal tower forming a vertical axis. Although the forms he used were distinctly Constructivist, Gabo's project, like Mendelsohn's, seems to have been inspired by the Expressionist motif of the "Stadt-krone" which Bruno Taut had launched just after the First World War and which reappears in most examples of large-scale architecture designed or built in Eastern and Central Europe between the wars.

However different the plastic idioms they bring into play, these three remarkable projects show a common concern for an immediately perceptible unity of design, formal continuity and outline. It is through the cohesion and density of the plastic block formed by interlocking volumes that the edifice acquires a monumental significance. This is not the case with the fourth project, the one drawn up by Le Corbusier. Here one cannot speak of any unity or synthesis of form; the very idea of an edifice seems to be set at naught. Volumes are not only broken up according to their functions, in the manner of Constructivism; they are literally taken apart and spaced out over a scattered plan, one that remains in the mind rather as a movement or a rhythm. "To signify by art the epic conquest of the new age," wrote Le Corbusier. For the movements of the crowd, hero of that conquest, he provided amply in the circulation channels of his spacious plan; indeed, acting in the spirit of the revolutionary celebrations of 1918 and in that of the contemporary Soviet cinema, Le Corbusier left it to these crowd movements, it would seem, to create that unity which the other projects sought to attain by the play of architectural forms. The "machinery" of his design, which traditional-minded critics chose to stigmatize as inhuman, thus made a larger allowance for man than did other less aggressively Constructivist compositions. It should be noted moreover that Le Corbusier refrained from substituting the movement of the machine for the movement of human masses, as Tatlin had done.

Sketch of a Sea Shell.

effect he gives the idea of the free plan a new dimension, the time dimension: to the initial cell, or room, can be added as desired any number of prefabricated cells ("a column, a beam, a ceiling element, a lighting element") detached from the ground and lighted from above. This method allowed of "unlimited growth": the freedom of the plan became a freedom of evolution. And though the envelope hitherto containing the "organs" had now completely disappeared, the "unit" remained under what Le Corbusier would have called its "biological" aspect, for the extension of the spiral plan always remained organically linked to a single center or focal point.

Such is not the case with the Swiss Pavilion, and even less with the project for the Palace of the Soviets. In both, the volumes are set over against each other with an apparently total freedom. Here Le Corbusier explores another dimension of freedom, one that in academic terms may be called composition. The "organs" corresponding to the different functions are treated as independent plastic units, and thus the architecture itself is organized as a site, as a landscape, and an increasingly complex one. The "inside" becomes an "outside." Here begins the transition from architecture to town-planning.

It was during the 1920's, when he was working out a new organization of the living area, of the cells (as he called the rooms), that Le Corbusier developed the idea of the free plan: its purpose was to give the dweller a maximum of freedom within the minimum space allotted to him by modern society. From 1930 on, after the brilliant prelude of his designs for the League of Nations building and the World City, he transposed into large apartment buildings the experience he had gained on the level of the individual "living unit." Three large studies, roughly contemporary with one another, mark this transition: the two projects for a Museum of Modern Art and the Palace of the Soviets, and the Swiss Pavilion at the Cité Universitaire in Paris.

In its rigorous logic and its wealth of invention, the project for a Museum of Modern Art illustrates Le Corbusier's unrivaled ability to reduce any architectural program to a basic principle capable of a variety of applications. Here in

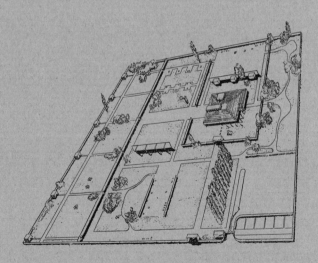

Project for the Museum of Unlimited Growth, 1931.

Model of the Museum of Unlimited Growth, 1931.

Project for a University City, 1925.

From the 1925 plan of a University City to the Venice Hospital of 1965, by way of the Museum project of 1930 which he took up again and again, there runs a direct line of filiation: they all exemplify, on the level of large-scale planning, that process of continuous invention by successive enrichments of the original idea which characterizes all of Le Corbusier's creative work. Principles defined in connection with programs planned out only on the most general lines (University City, Museum of Modern Art) ultimately yield the exact solution to the problem set by a particular case or a unique site, whose requirements have to be combined with those of a complex program very different from the programs which gave rise to the original researches. But this solution itself, far from being a final result or a special application devoid of general import, opens up new possibilities—which Le Corbusier, in this particular case, did not have time to explore himself.

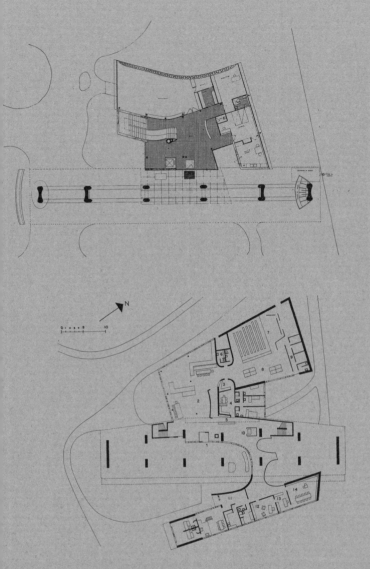

A comparison between the ground-floor plans of the Swiss and Brazilian Pavilions (both being closely related) on the one hand and the Venice Hospital on the other brings out the contrasting uses made by Le Corbusier in his large-scale buildings of the freedom of the plan. In the two pavilions of the Cité Universitaire, we find a dynamic equilibrium based on the counterpoint of strongly diversified plastic masses, disposed without reference to any regulating grid. In Venice, we find a horizontal expansion, spreading steadily outward but controlled by a modular grid fixing the directions and rhythm of growth, further extension being made easy by the use of standardized units. The pilotis gain an added interest and usefulness when the architect has to deal with volumes covering a wide surface area, for they enable him not only to do away with view-blocking walls at ground level and straight-line traffic lanes, but to create an architectural landscape of great richness and variety by means of contrasting lights and shadows, contrasting full and empty spaces, at the eye level of the pedestrian. Here was a singularly effective means of visually characterizing the urban itineraries.

Swiss Pavilion at the Cité Universitaire, Paris, 1930-1932.
Plan of the ground floor.

Brazilian Pavilion at the Cité Universitaire, Paris, 1957-1959.
Plan of the ground floor.

Project for the Hospital in Venice, 1965.
Bird's-eye view of the model.

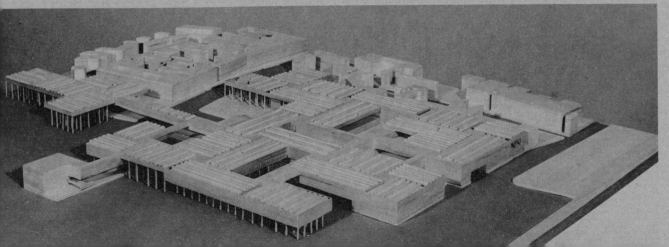

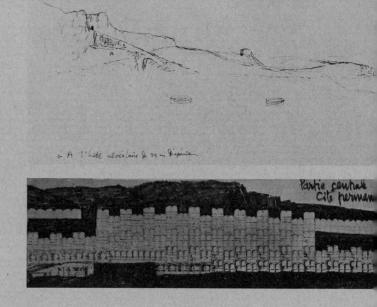

The rather romantic project of 1948 for a pilgrimage center at La Sainte-Baume, near Marseilles, included an underground basilica and a "permanent city" to be erected on the mountainside; the plans of the latter were taken up and amplified the following year for a program of vacation housing at Cap-Martin on the French Riviera (Rob and Roq projects, unexecuted). Both at Sainte-Baume and Cap-Martin, the problem was to adapt to a steeply sloping site, whose line had to be respected, the system of collective housing deriving from the principles laid down in connection with the multistory villas (immeubles-villas) and applied to the Marseilles apartment block (Unité d'Habitation) then under construction: complete visual and acoustic insulation of the apartments, natural conditions (space, sun, greenery), and communal services.

Nearly twenty years before, in the huge viaduct apartment buildings which he devised in his town-planning schemes for Rio de Janeiro and Algiers, Le Corbusier had shown that, while he meant to keep to these principles, the form of the "instrument" embodying them could differ considerably from the theoretical scheme which he was laying down at the same period in the Radiant City. At Sainte-Baume and Cap-Martin, the need to adapt the project to the site led to much more than a transformation of the architectural instrument; it led to abandonment of the very idea of form, to a transition to a "formless" architecture. The large vertical slab, opposing its prismatic mass to the uncontrolled caprice of natural forms, here gave way to an outspread structure strictly governed by those natural forms; furthermore, neither the dimensions (that is, the number of apartments grouped together) nor the internal articulation of this structure are determined in advance or taken over from one project to the other. This flexibility gives the apartment an autonomy so marked that buildings of this type can no longer be called collective, but only semi-collective, dwellings.

It is characteristic of Le Corbusier's logic, or, if one will, of his contradictoriness, that he invented these "stepped clusters" of contiguous dwellings at the very time when, in response to attacks levelled against the Marseilles apartment block, he undertook to justify the large vertical slab-type apartment building by a categorical generalization. The Sainte-Baume and Cap-Martin projects represent the outcome and conclusion of twenty-five years' work, and the fact that they never got beyond the planning stage and, even at that stage, aroused violent opposition has obscured the importance of these designs, which not only open up new perspectives but have the added interest of summarizing Le Corbusier's architectural views at that time.

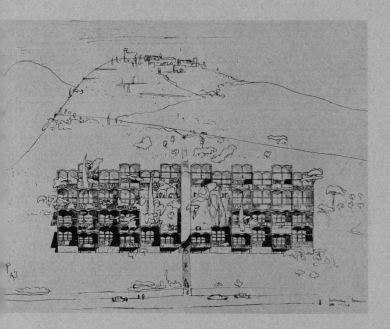

In his plans for apartment blocks and offices, Le Corbusier was to emphasize the unity of the prism resulting from repetition of the individual "squares" (in the southern French term for room, *carrée*, Le Corbusier claimed to find confirmation of the "law of the right angle"). Elongated, in bar form, in the Swiss Pavilion, the apartment blocks, or the Secretariat in Chandigarh; upright, in tower form, in the model for the United Nations; or dilated, in rhomboid form, under the pressure of interior traffic ways, as in the Rentenanstalt and the different versions of the skyscraper in Algiers (the suggestion did not pass unnoticed: witness, amongst numerous examples, the Pirelli Tower in Milan), the prism seemed to assert itself once and for all for every multicellular type of building: the interplay of proportions alone determined its equilibrium.

At the same time, Le Corbusier was careful not to introduce into the prism anything which, within these very programs, was not repetitive. The Swiss Pavilion provides the first and probably the most perfect example of a formula which was to achieve world-wide success. The "chest" of the Pavilion containing the rooms, representing the "repetition of *carrées*," detached from the soil by *pilotis*, contrasts with the flexible forms of the non-standardized offices: reception hall, conference room, manager's quarters. The stairway tower itself is projected outside the prism, a solution which, in Chandigarh, served to break up the monotony of the long western façade of the Secretariat. In the Salvation Army hostel in Paris, the contrasted masses of the reception hall are likewise placed in front of the glass walls of the dormitory building.

In the most spectacular project of the 1930's, however, the relationship between the dominant prism and the free secondary masses is reversed. In fact, the program for the Palace of the Soviets accorded more importance to the organs of communal life (assembly halls and traffic ways) than to the multicellular elements (offices). The machine aesthetic is here expressed in an all-out solution which lays bare all the organs, shaped solely by the laws of fluid dynamics (traffic ways) and acoustics (halls), and then assembles them like the parts of a motor. Compared with this gigantic piece of machinery, the other, rival projects—and even the Centrosoyuz in Moscow, which Le Corbusier designed and built

Sketch from the Travel Notebooks, 1908?

more or less simultaneously, and which is nonetheless articulated like a fine piece of mechanical engineering—produce an impression of neoclassical restraint and sobriety. But whereas Tatlin, facing the same program, recalled the Eiffel Tower, Le Corbusier himself, by his own admission, drew his inspiration from the Campo Santo in Pisa.

This search for a "synthetic solution," by assembling organs shaped independently of one another, evidently derived from the same approach that had determined the concept of the "living-machine." The analytical attitude which it presupposed was to call in question the very prism itself. Ever since 1933, the way had been paved for the break-up of the prism by projects for linear dwellings in tiers (the Durand allotment for Algiers). In the projects of the immediate post-war period (Sainte-Baume, Rob and Roq), each "square" recovered its freedom, and the cells stuck together in an amorphous "crust" upon the slope. One naturally recalls the Cité Universitaire of 1925, but here all formal or dimensional definition was abandoned; the agglomeration could grow by free proliferation, heedless of any envelope. Le Corbusier himself was not to realize any of these projects, but the numerous examples of the honeycomb solution for accommodation in tiers (both natural and artificial) achieved during the last fifteen years provide ample proof of its fertility. In addition to, and independently of, the Unité d'Habitation (apartment building), these projects define a type of semi-collective housing fraught with possibilities, and it is to Le Corbusier that the credit for first exploring the idea properly belongs.

The years 1950-1965—which, together with the decade 1925-1935, represent the periods in Le Corbusier's career most rich in architectural invention—

witnessed the development of widely varying themes in the sphere of the plan: a return to the unit of the square, at La Tourette, at Ahmedabad, at Strasbourg, in the church in Firminy and above all the Assembly Hall in Chandigarh, which in this respect represents the exact counterpart of the Palace of the Soviets; decomposition of the mass, on the lines of the Swiss Pavilion, in the Brazilian Pavilion and the Olivetti Center; finally, honeycomb structures, in the hospital in Venice and, most probably, in the project—no more than a rough sketch at the time of Le Corbusier's death—for the Twentieth Century Museum in Nanterre. Depending on the program and the site, he imbricated the "organs" within the unit of a block, individualized them in the form of "plastic objects" linked by strict proportional ratios, or allowed the cells to proliferate in apparent freedom.

The most striking factor in the revision of the plastic idiom during the 1930's was the introduction of the sun-break *(brise-soleil)*. Added to the "five points" of 1925 as a sort of "redeeming section," one finds it, in one form or another, in almost all the projects conceived after 1933. The white screens and glass walls, stretched like a diaphanous film around the "organs" of the living-machine, now disappear behind a mask of concrete slabs perpendicular to the plane of the façade. The envelope seems to lose all its transparency, the façade all its freedom. However marked the plastic nature of the sun-break—as in the central part of the Secretariat in Chandigarh—this counted for less than its permeability and susceptibility to variations in light. Le Corbusier treats the sun-break both as an extension of the interior masses (which he protects not only from the sun's rays but also from too brutal a contact with the

Staircase in Le Corbusier's Apartment at 24, rue Nungesser-et-Coli, Paris, 1933. (Photograph taken during the artist's lifetime).

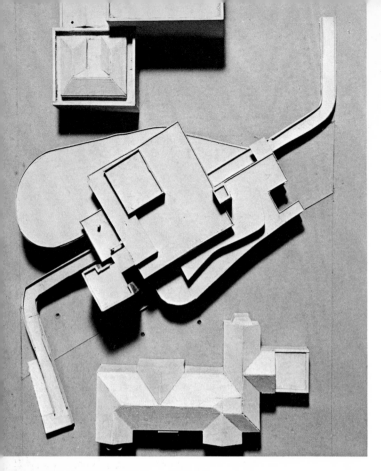

The Secretariat at Chandigarh (Punjab), 1958. ►
Ramps seen from the terrace-roof.

◄ *Carpenter Center for the Visual Arts, Harvard University,*
Cambridge, Mass., 1961-1964.
Bird's-eye view of the model showing the design adopted
for circulation.

Plan of the Secretariat at Chandigarh showing the layout
of the ramps projecting beyond the prism of the building.
▼

*Le Corbusier always admired the wide variety of structural
arrangements resorted to in folk architecture to solve the
problem of passing from one level to another—a problem
professional architects have not always coped with very
successfully. Because it required the least amount of space,
and also because it enriched the "architectural promenade"
with a turning movement of great visual interest, Le Corbusier had a preference for the winding staircase, of which he
produced a great many free interpretations. One of the most
flexible is the inner staircase he designed for his own
apartment in Paris. He avoided straight flights of stairs
and replaced them by ramps with a low angle of slope, which
create an almost imperceptible gliding movement from level
to level. It is interesting to note, too, that, quite apart from
the ramps, the passageways in Le Corbusier's architecture
are often laid out along a very slight incline, so slight that
it passes unnoticed in photographs and small-scale plans.
With him, this was no doubt a device of optical correction,
but it was also an effective means of diversifying the
muscular experience of the architectural promenade.*

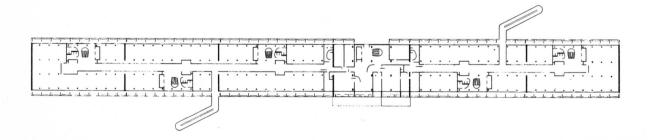

outside world) and as a penetration of exterior space into the very mass of the building. This penetration in turn makes it possible to deaden, without weakening, the shock of the encounter between interior mass and exterior light: in the multicellular buildings, where it appears as part of a regular texture, the sun-break thus becomes the instrument of a paradoxical restoration of the surface. In fact, its texture enables it both to capture and channel the light in flexible form and to distribute it with regularity. The surface, though its unity is restored, now becomes porous, and so absorbs and reflects the light, continually modifying its aspect according to the time of day and the movements of the spectator; it thus regains, albeit in very different plastic guise, the mobility and transparency of the earlier Purist membrane. When, as in the loggias in Marseilles, the lateral faces of the vertical slabs are colored, or when, as in Ahmedabad, Harvard, or the Assembly Hall in Chandigarh, the slabs are arranged obliquely in relation to the glass wall, the resultant effect of instability is sufficiently powerful to bring to life masses which, judged by the mere cubic content of the material utilized, seem to exclude all idea of mobility or metamorphosis. The "play of forms in light" is here realized in at once the most literal and most sensitive of manners. It is only through light, and the movement of light, that the forms come to life, and, through them, the space also.

◀ *Dominican Monastery of La Tourette at Eveux, near Lyons, 1956-1959.*
Corridor leading to the church, with undulatory glass wall.

Dominican Monastery of La Tourette at Eveux, near Lyons, ▶
1956-1959. Corridor.

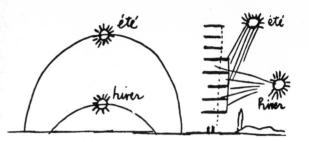

Sketch of the "Redeeming Section," showing the need for sun-control louvers adjustable according to the position of the sun.

The brise-soleil, or sun-break, is generally regarded as Le Corbusier's most characteristic contribution to architecture during the last twenty years of his life, just as the concept of pilotis, or stilts, lifting a building off the ground and liberating the space beneath it, was the most significant feature of his early work. The sun-break was a product of the free façade: in conjunction with the glass wall, it provided what he called la coupe salvatrice (the redeeming section). Like the pilotis, it took a variety of forms, according to the changing requirements of programs and sites, and these varying forms count for much in the renewal of what has been wrongly called Le Corbusier's "style". From the "parasol" of the Carthage villa to that of the Palace of Justice at Chandigarh, from the laminated sun-breaks of Rio to the "undulatory glass wall" of La Tourette, the distance is considerable, but the differences between them answer to a rigorous logic. Like the pilotis, the sun-break became the instrument of a more and more poetic trans-position of its original function: the light-wall of Ronchamp and the undulatory glass wall create, between the daily round indoors and the seasonal cycle of the sun, a link of the same nature as that created in medieval architecture by the colored light of the stained-glass window.

Ministry of Education, Rio de Janeiro, 1936.
Sun-breaks on the north façade.

The Marseilles Apartment Building, 1945-1952. Loggias. ▶

Dominican Monastery of La Tourette at Eveux, near Lyons, 1956-1959. The altar of the Holy Sacrament.

◄ *Page 136: The Palace of Justice (Law Courts) at Chandigarh (Punjab), 1956. Sun-breaks on the east façade.*

◄ *Page 137: Church of Ronchamp, near Belfort, 1950-1953. The south wall ("light-wall") seen from inside.*

Vigorously though he asserted the mechanical character of the forms employed, Le Corbusier had refused to treat the Palace of the Soviets as a symbolic figuration: he saw it as a meeting place of decision-makers on whom the fate of millions depended, and he designed it to accompany and facilitate their deliberations. In the same way, he did not take the Tourette monastery as a pretext for expressing an abstract idea or a mystical aspiration, nor did he make it answer to any predetermined form or system of forms. He viewed this Dominican monastery as a machine whose purpose was to enable a hundred men to live together in a community governed by rule—men who, by study and meditation, were preparing themselves for action. The rule itself laid down the essential part of the program: a balanced alternation of times of work and prayer, of solitude and forgathering. Hence the key importance of exactly defining the relations between places of individual retreat and places of collective celebration, "of contacts and circuits." The need for such places, together with a necessary regard for the nature of the site, represented the determining factor in the choice of a design which is monumental and closed only in appearance.

Dominican Monastery of La Tourette at Eveux, near Lyons, 1956-1959. Overall view from the southwest.

Who, then, was Le Corbusier the architect? Neither Purist painter in Poissy nor Baroque poet in Ronchamp. Far from threatening the permanency of his underlying theme of liberty of plan and envelope ("free plan," "free façade"), the choice and renewal of "plastic tools" appear rather as its consequences. True, the fluidity and continuity of space are commonplaces in the architectural thought of the twentieth century; but what sets Le Corbusier's experiments apart within this movement, what lends his work a dramatic tension essentially his own, is the vigor, the almost Michelangelesque violence, with which this dynamic approach to space gives rise to forms so powerfully characterized that it seems condemned to find its further progress blocked by them, and yet ultimately it always manages to throw them off and outstrip them.

True, the concretization of plastic form assumes, with Le Corbusier, the character of a veritable fatality; but one also finds a no less constant

"Architecture, which in its substance and texture is immanent mathematics, has the same radiation as that possessed by the functions of curves and straight lines. Around the building and inside the building, there are precise places, mathematical places, which integrate the whole and which are tribunes whence the speaking voice will find its echo all around. These are the places of sculpture. And by this is meant neither metope nor tympanum nor porch, but something much more subtle and precise. They are places which are like the focal point of a parabola or an ellipse, like the exact spot where the different planes composing the architectural landscape intersect. Places that are speaking-tubes, mouthpieces, loudspeakers." Such was Le Corbusier's conception of Ronchamp—in 1935.

Church of Ronchamp, near Belfort, 1950-1953.
View of the east façade and choir.

Church of Ronchamp,
near Belfort,
1950-1953.
Southeast corner.

*The Philips Pavilion
at the Brussels
World's Fair, 1958.*

determination to treat that form only as a "tool": however vigorously he may articulate it, form, for Le Corbusier, is never a means of expression in itself, but an instrument of invention within space and the fruit of the latter.

This singular tension between the form and the movement of space can already be sensed in the buildings of the 1920's. In his post-1950 creations, it produced those mutations in the plastic idiom—for example, from orthogonal planes to freely articulated curved surfaces—which led to the belief, more especially with regard to Ronchamp and the Philips Pavilion, that Le Corbusier was repudiating that strict discipline whose symbol, for him, the right angle had become. In reality, however, it was merely a question of creating the most flexible possible envelope and one that should be best capable of embracing the movement of a highly characterized interior space. The fact is that, in the case of both Ronchamp and the Philips Pavilion, the form of the envelope was determined by "acoustic" considerations—literally in the Philips Pavilion, for it was the scene of a total audio-visual spectacle,

the "Electronic Poem"; figuratively in the Ronchamp chapel. It was with reference to the latter that Le Corbusier coined the expression "landscape acoustics," often made use of since. But equally important at Ronchamp was his desire to blind the eye to the real size of the chapel, which is quite small, by a play of curved surfaces, and by fully exploiting these optical adjustments to arouse a sense of "ineffable space."

For Le Corbusier, whether he asserted the order-giving power of the right angle or developed non-Euclidean suggestions in apparent freedom, a given system of organizing space was no more an immutable entity endowed with intrinsic virtues than was a given form. In so far as they permitted him to execute the forms elaborated by the progress of "liberating technics," he overlooked none of the contemporary hypotheses on the structure of plastic space: from the geometrizing simultaneity of Cubism to the grid-space of the first explorers of the purely visual and to the dynamic topology of Delaunay and Kandinsky, Le Corbusier seems to have assimilated and experienced them all simultaneously.

From Architecture to Town-Planning

Only a revolution in town-planning
can create the conditions
necessary for a revolution
in art and housing.

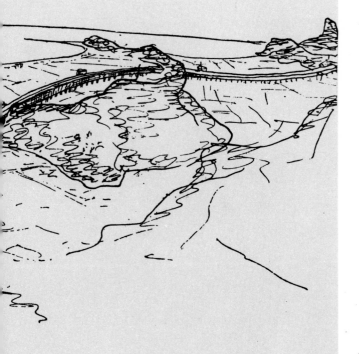

Town-Planning Study for Rio de Janeiro, 1929-1930.
Fragment. Pen drawing.

FROM ARCHITECTURE TO TOWN-PLANNING

From the living-machine to the Palace of the Soviets, from the cabin at Cap-Martin to the Capitol in Chandigarh, from the "elementary" program of an individual cell multipliable *ad infinitum* to the Piranesian complex in which the will of the collectivity finds elaboration and expression, Le Corbusier apparently remained faithful to the selfsame method of creation: "In the different stages of the project," he said of the Palace of the Soviets, "one sees the organs, already shaped independently of one another, gradually taking up their respective positions, to culminate in a synthetic solution." Two decades later, the civic center in Saint-Dié again brought together organs "shaped independently of one another": administrative center, museum, community house, hotel, shops, and so on. The project seems to illustrate the application of that same mechanical "way of thinking" on a scale that surpasses mere architecture and already embraces town-planning.

The living-machine resulted from the assembly of "organs" whose forms and relations were defined with an objective exactitude which Le Corbusier never tired of emphasizing (in practice, the open

character of the plans and the constant invention of new forms fortunately tempered the rigor of these standards). In his view, the same method could be applied in town-planning, not only to dense multifunctional ensembles, as in the case of the core of the town, but to the complete city as an entity. It is at the architectural level that town-planning begins. For each of the functions of the town, a suitable "organ" or tool must be created: "The tools of town-planning will take on the form of living architectural units, each characterized by a biological exactitude that is alone capable of fulfilling the tasks involved." The demand for "biological exactitude" suggests that the organs and standards are "open," i.e. that they are conceived of as being complementary to one another and are established on the same scale, corresponding to one and the same "order of size." An organ does not function in isolation but only within the context of an organism: there can be no architecture without town-planning. Conversely, just as there can be no organization without pre-existing organs, a form of town-planning which did not have a complete "set of tools" at its disposal would remain theoretical and inoperative. There can be no town-planning without architecture: "Architecture in all things, town-planning in all things."

In this assimilation of architecture and town-planning, it is interesting to note the part played by the mechanical metaphor on the one hand and the concept of standard on the other. It was this concept, in Le Corbusier's eyes, which reconciled the classical demand for universal solutions with the technical demand for standardization: of one of the standards of the living-machine, the roof-garden, Le Corbusier wrote that it was an "event of a technical order, and *consequently of universal value...*" The universality of technics permitted and justified the use of "standard equipment." Beginning in 1922, the project for *immeuble-villas* (apartment blocks consisting of superimposed villas) — from which, twenty-five years later, the Unité d'Habitation or Housing Unit was to emerge — provided a typical example of the manner in which Le Corbusier understood an integrated architectural tool, an "instrument of urban renovation." The arrangement of the cells in the form of a "vertical garden-city" also provided the urban space (in which it acquired its full value) with that same conquest of the third dimension which simultaneously asserted itself, at the architectural level, in the interior organization of the cells. The organic coherence of the structure of architectural space and urban space was thus assured, still on the basis of the mechanical analogy, as well as the mutual independence of the living quarters and the traffic ways. Moreover, the very extensive communal services with which Le Corbusier intended to equip the Villa Apartment Blocks were designed not only to constitute "extensions of the living quarters" which would relieve the cell of certain functions that could be better realized on the collective rather than the individual plane (automatic laundry, servicing staff, centralized watering system for the loggia-gardens)

Sketch showing the Position of the Church of Santa Giustina, ▶
Venice, in relation to the adjacent Square, 1915 (?).
Drawn from old prints.

Camillo Sitte (1843-1903). ▶
Piazza dei Signori and Palladio's Basilica at Vicenza.
Piazza del Duomo and Piazza del Papa at Perugia.
("a" indicates the Palazzo Comunale)

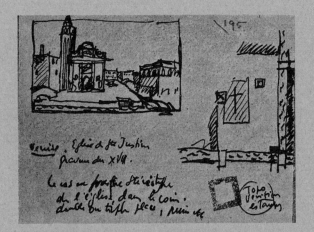

The social thinkers of the second half of the nineteenth century, anxious to improve the living conditions of the working classes, drew up many programs for the construction of workers' housing. But none of these programs seems to have made any allowance for the specific character of the urban problem as a whole. It was only towards the end of the century that two studies appeared, very different from each other, which proposed a comprehensive interpretation of the subject: Der Städtebau nach seinen künstlerischen Grundsätzen by the Viennese Camillo Sitte, who adopted a strictly aesthetic point of view, and Garden Cities of To-morrow by the Englishman Ebenezer Howard, whose attitude was resolutely social. It was the reading of these pioneer books, whose views and proposals he later violently condemned, that set Le Corbusier seriously thinking about town-planning problems.

Camillo Sitte he later regarded as the man responsible for the international vogue of picturesque urbanism, applying to the moribund old town, and to the modern town, too, with all its uncertainties, a purely cosmetic treatment in the medieval style. He accused Sitte of senselessly initiating the cult of what he liked to call the "donkey path":

"Man walks straight because he has a goal: he knows where he's going. He has decided to go somewhere, and he walks straight there.

"The donkey zigzags and dawdles, absent-mindedly, zigzagging to keep clear of the big stones, to evade sloping ground, to get into the shade: he takes the least possible pains.

"Man rules his feelings by the thinking mind: he curbs his feelings and instincts in favor of the aim he has before him. He controls his beast by his intelligence...

"To produce, you must have a line of conduct: you must obey the rules of experience. You have got to think ahead, to the result.

"The donkey thinks of nothing at all, only of not bothering. The donkey has laid out all the cities on the continent, including Paris, unfortunately...

"The religion of the donkey path has just been set up.

"The movement started in Germany, the result of a wrong-headed book by Camillo Sitte on town-planning, glorifying the curve and demonstrating its peerless beauties. Proof of this is seen in all the art cities of the Middle Ages: the author has confused the picturesque and pictorial with the rules governing a city's vitality...

"An appalling and paradoxical mistake, in the day of the automobile. 'So much the better,' said a town councillor to me, 'the cars won't be able to run any more.'

"The curving street is the way for donkeys, the straight street is the way for men."

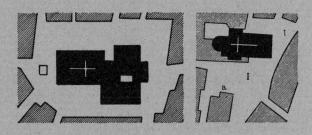

It seems quite likely, nevertheless, that it was from Sitte that Le Corbusier learned to see the city in its entirety as an architectural landscape, as a site; and this way of seeing he practised in his early travels and later developed systematically by a study of the topographical collections in the Bibliothèque Nationale in Paris. It was no doubt Sitte too who developed in him a sense of the historical reality of the city as a tissue of pathways—both for donkeys and men. But, unlike Sitte, Le Corbusier did not see in its ways and streets merely a sequence of more or less picturesque "sights": for him they constituted the circulatory system of an organism which could not live without them.

Le Corbusier's debt to the theorists of the garden-city is equally certain and no less ambiguous. Of course he spoke out against the danger of "de-urbanization" which the garden-cities represented, for they proposed a false solution to the problem of the city and could only lead to "a sterile isolation of the individual," whom they would maintain in "a slavery organized by capitalist society." As he fought against the "corridor-street" and the slums it gives rise to, so he fought against the "great illusion" of the individual home, taking up space and generating circulation. To the horizontal garden-city he opposed as early as 1922 his large, regenerated apartment building, his vertical garden-city. This apartment block, consisting in essence of superimposed villas, this immeuble-villa as he called it, reduced distances and facilitated social contacts and integration of the different urban functions. But whether the dwellings were grouped vertically or horizontally, it was still a garden-city, and it is the same "essential joys" promised by Howard and his friends towards which sails, above the trees of the green belt, the great concrete ship of the apartment block which he called the Unité d'Habitation, the housing unit.

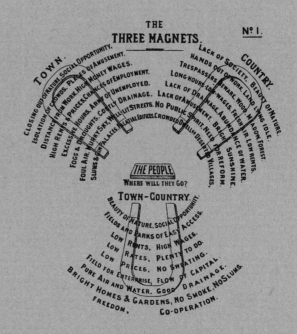

Ebenezer Howard (1850-1928).
"The Three Magnets."

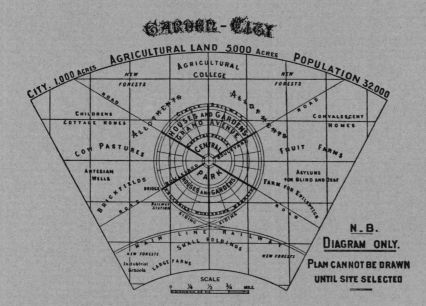

Diagram of a Garden City
with its Rural Belt.

The connections between Tony Garnier's Industrial City and Le Corbusier's Contemporary City are less ambiguous. The latter owes much to its precursor: the functional zoning, the independence and continuity of the pedestrian ways in particular. It differs radically from it in size (a population of three million instead of 30,000) and in its program (a change-over city and not a center of production), but not in spirit or method. Garnier's Industrial City was the first comprehensive and coherent town-planning proposition that Le Corbusier met on his way, and it contributed decisively to his own approach to town-planning.

Tony Garnier (1869-1948).
Project for an Industrial City, 1901-1904:
Residential District and Plan of the City Center.

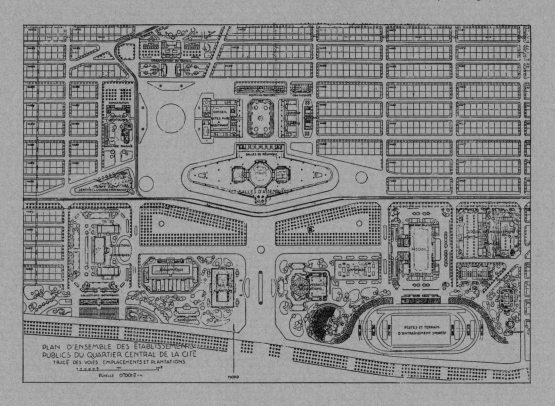

Project for Multistory Villas (Immeuble-Villas):
Above: Apartment Block of 120 Superimposed Villas, 1922.
Below: Detail of the Villa Apartment Block.
"The usual module of the façades (3¹/₂ meters) is carried to
6 meters, giving the street a wholly new breadth and sweep."

The type of apartment building composed of multistory villas, which Le Corbusier called immeuble-villas, combined the new distribution of the living area as exemplified in the Citrohan house (two-story living room and hanging garden) with the advantages procured by highly developed common services. Several variants of this apartment building were studied, either on the open plan forming an indented pattern or on a closed plan extending around a vast central courtyard. The Immeuble Clarté in Geneva, or Glass House as it is called locally, is a reduced version of a much larger project (Wanner Buildings) which was never carried out. The apartments stand on two levels, the living room having a double floor height over part of its surface. Together with the Salvation Army hostel and the rue Nungesser-et-Coli apartment house in Paris, and the Centrosoyuz in Moscow, the Immeuble Clarté is one of the buildings in which Le Corbusier made the most extensive use of glass walls.

Apartment Building in Geneva (Immeuble Clarté), ▶
1930-1932. (Photograph taken in 1932)

but also to exert a renovating influence on the structure of the city itself: for instance, cooperative shopping centers would have rendered the central market halls superfluous. More important than the detail of the arrangements envisaged was the determination to forge a concrete link, through a permanent series of exchanges, between the cell and the city, the city and the cell: "Architecture in all things, town-planning in all things."

The extrapolation of the organ concept at town-planning level came, in Le Corbusier's case, long before the drawing-up of a precise inventory of the functions these organs were intended to discharge. The famous nomenclature of the Athens Charter coincides only partly with the "urban tools" which he himself elaborated. In fact his most advanced studies, like his large-scale town-planning projects, are centered exclusively on three functions, or groups of functions: housing, traffic, and administration; industrial production was not integrated until much later—later even than agricultural production. As for the "cultivation of mind and body" referred to in the Charter, it certainly provided Le Corbusier with a theme for projects as numerous as they were spectacular; but they had nothing of the systematic character of the studies devoted to housing or circulation, and it was not until the plan for Saint-Dié that the main elements of cultural equipment were allotted a clearly defined place inside the city.

The "tools" corresponding to the major functions were defined in detail and continually revised. As regards housing, the projects for vertical collective dwellings, from multistory villas *(immeuble-villas)*, honeycomb developments *(lotissements à alvéoles)*, and indented apartment blocks *(immeubles à redents)* to the various versions of the Unité d'Habitation,

should not blind us to studies undertaken in other directions, such as the linear residence in tiers or horizontal semi-collective dwellings. The "tools" devised by Le Corbusier in this sphere were not confined, as some often profess to believe, to the Unité d'Habitation alone: witness the countless architects who took their inspiration from one or other motif of the continuous dwelling which Le Corbusier did not have the chance of developing himself.

As for studies on traffic, these go back to the summary classification, inspired by Tony Garnier and other precursors, which we find in the "City for Three Million Inhabitants" (Ville Contemporaine); they were subsequently developed and diversified in the project for a "Radiant City" (Ville Radieuse) and the town-planning projects of the 1930's, and culminated in the complete "7 V" system applied in Chandigarh. The enormous cruciform skyscrapers in the business center which formed the core of the Ville Contemporaine subsequently evolved and found more exact expression in the two formulas, since become classical, of the tower with a lozenge-shaped plan (Rentenanstalt, Algiers skyscraper) and the three-pointed star (Cartesian skyscraper). By contrast, the study of the "instruments" of industrial production long remained sketchy: particularly remarkable is the clear-cut emphasis accorded to internal circulation pathways, first in the "standard workshops" of the Radiant City, then in the Green Factory, and finally in the Olivetti project.

As for the cultural "tools," their development remained strangely but significantly uneven: it would seem that the mood of the man and the whim of the

The Marseilles Apartment Block (Unité d'Habitation), ▶
1945-1952. West Front.

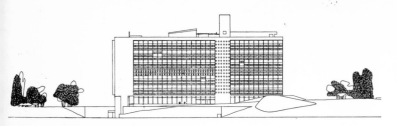

Design for the Berlin Apartment Block
(Unité d'Habitation), 1958.
Built only in part from Le Corbusier's plans.

artist here got the better of the logic of the theorist. The Museum, understood not in the traditional sense of a conservatory for works of art but as a "museum of knowledge," a permanent and encyclopedic center of audio-visual information, became the object of loving attention and development. For the theatrical arts, he devised some highly original arrangements, such as the "Miracle Box" and the "Spontaneous Theater." The inspiration of the "magnificent spectacle of grandeur, of unity, experienced... at the Vélodrome d'Hiver track," during the six-day bicycle races, in the company of Fernand Léger, and repeated periodically from the very windows of his apartment overlooking the Jean-Bouin Stadium, fired him with enthusiasm for grandiose solutions: at the time of the Popular Front, for the "Recreation Center for 100,000 Persons" and, in his later years, for a Stadium in Baghdad. But one is struck by the total absence of studies dealing with educational programs: apart from the day nurseries of the Unités in Marseilles and in Nantes (La Tourette was treated less as a Theological Faculty than as a unit of community life), the only project of this kind left by Le Corbusier was that for a University City in Rio, and even that

was more an excursion in town-planning than the study of an educational problem. Was this the instinctive mistrust of the self-taught man towards all schooling, a deeply rooted aversion to all learning acquired from books or lectures? Le Corbusier was nothing if not tenacious, and this was true even in the grudges he bore. Was it not the shocked recollection of the bazaar in Istanbul, explored twenty-five years earlier, that led him to omit all place for retail shopkeepers from his Radiant City?

Beginning with the studies in "agrarian renovation" which, during the thirties, completed those in "urban renovation" formulated ten years before, Le Corbusier progressively applied the same instrumentalist method to the whole complex of problems posed by the organization of the space occupied by man. It was not only the town that had been affected by the revolution of the machine; the traditional structures of the village had been undermined even more seriously: the peasant, like the town-dweller, had become a full-time member of industrial society. Just as he rejected an urbanism of picturesque or sentimental intimations, so Le Corbusier turned his back on the romantic aura of the old-world village: the "tools" which he proposed for its regeneration, inspired by examples of rural colonization observed in South America and in the Soviet Union, were the "radiant farm" and the cooperative organization of what he was later to call "the unit of agricultural production."

It was in the "cooperative village" that an entire "human establishment" was for the first time treated globally like a "tool," a standard. Ten years later, in his "Three Human Establishments," Le Corbusier was to define in categorical terms the three standards for the "occupation of territory" in industrial civilization. After the 1922 project, it was to the "radio-concentric change-over metropolis," as the grand center of decisions, administration, and business, that he was to devote all his care and attention. Secondary function was here eliminated, and was taken over by the "linear industrial city" stretching in a thin band, from metropolis to metropolis, along the main transportation arteries. Finally, set apart from these arteries but not far from them, the pinpoint "unit of agricultural production," thanks to intensive mechanization, would enable the best land to be exploited in rational fashion by a small staff of technicians. To these three establishments should be added the "nature preserve" which, quantitatively speaking, included the major part of the land; this would not be left to run wild but would be arranged to provide for leisure pursuits—leisure, in Le Corbusier's eyes, being the one function for which space neither could nor should be spared.

Between the articles in *L'Esprit Nouveau*, in which Le Corbusier had first formulated his theory of the standard, and the definition of the Three Human Establishments, twenty-five years had gone by. The extrapolation was thus accomplished very slowly, and was, moreover, conducted—in countless writings, lectures, exhibitions, and diverse plans and projects—in a social and cultural context that had gradually undergone a radical transformation.

The first study, the Ville Contemporaine of 1922, had emerged against the background of the theories of the pre-war pioneers (Ebenezer Howard and his garden-city, Camillo Sitte and his *Städtebau nach seinen künstlerischen Grundsätzen*, Tony Garnier and the Industrial City), and of the first German experiments in *Siedlungen*. Reacting against the solutions proposed by his forerunners, which he condemned

Apartment Block (Unité d'Habitation) at Nantes-Rezé, 1953.

Apartment Block (Unité d'Habitation) at Briey-la-Forêt, 1959.

Apartment Block (Unité d'Habitation) at Firminy, 1968. Finished after Le Corbusier's death.

for their partial character and their failure to grasp the dimensions of the new age, Le Corbusier at once formulated, in comprehensive terms, the problem of the large city, master instrument of industrial civilization in its role of "center of decision" and living medium of the countless multitude. The aim of the study was twofold: to bring out in spectacular fashion the indissoluble link existing between the problems of large residential concentrations and intra-urban traffic, and to define the "order of size" of the tools to be used.

By the time, ten years later, that Le Corbusier was elaborating his second great theoretical study, the Radiant City, the situation had undergone a profound change: in Germany, Holland, France, and the Soviet Union, the problems of housing the largest possible number of people had given rise to numerous studies and agreement had been reached within the international movement on several major themes; the large city, regarded as the natural environment of an industrial civilization, had found impassioned theorists and supporters, who even included Mondrian. From 1928 onwards, CIAM (Congrès Internationaux de l'Architecture Moderne) had become the periodical forum for a vast confrontation on a European scale. It thus seemed that the time had come for a synthesis, placing the accent on what emerged as the most important outcome of CIAM's analysis: the "classification" of the multifunctional city into a system of zones.

As for the work of ASCORAL (Association de Constructeurs pour un Renouvellement Architectural), whose conclusions found expression in the Three Human Establishments, it was conducted in the context of the immense task of reconstruction which presented itself after the Second World War.

For Le Corbusier, the basic problem of all housing lies in the relationship between the individual and the collectivity. And so the first "instrument of urban renovation" that he set out to define was the one which would enable him to balance this relationship.

The problem is eternal; so the solution should be universal. "What are we dealing with? 800,000 or 200,000 or 3,000 inhabitants? By no means! We are dealing with a man, a woman and a few children, the elements of harmony in a home." The different versions of the Housing Unit (Unité d'Habitation), whether multistory villas or a block of flats on an indented plan, all start from the same postulate: "If you want to raise your family in privacy, silence, and natural conditions..." And they arrive at the solution exemplified for the first time at Marseilles: "... then join together with two thousand people and take each other by the hand; go through a single door and up in four elevators holding twenty people each... You will have seclusion, silence, and rapidity of 'inside-outside' contacts. Your houses will be 165 feet high... there will be parks around them for the recreation of children, adolescents, grown-ups. And on the roof you will have the most wonderful day nurseries."

Sketch for a Projected Apartment Block (Unité ▶
d'Habitation) in Algiers, 1942.
"The 24-hour cycle of the sun, the fundamental event which sets the rhythm of men's lives."

In black: the ground covered by an apartment block
(Unité d'Habitation) of 350 flats housing 1600 people.
In white: the ground covered by a horizontal garden city
housing the same number of people.

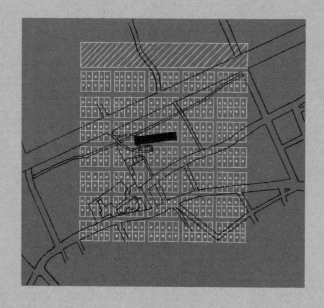

Project for Meaux:
Five Apartment Blocks (Unités d'Habitation)
and Two Towers for Bachelors, 1955-1960.

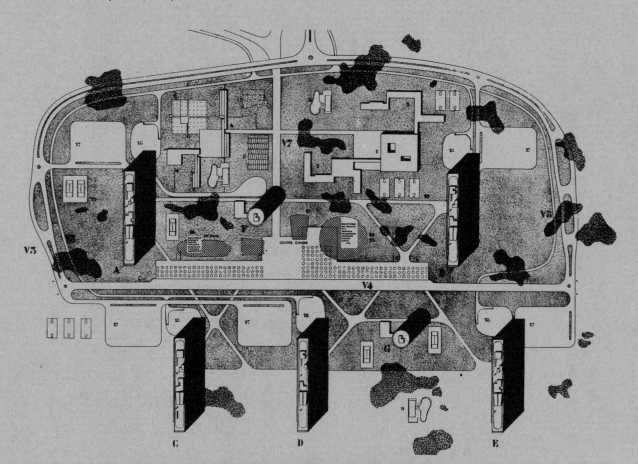

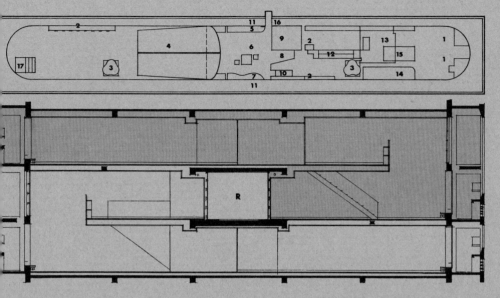

1. Artificial mountain range
2. Flower boxes
3. Ventilation shafts
4. Gymnasium
5. East solarium
6. Dressing room and upper terrace
7. West solarium
8. Concrete tables
9. Elevator tower with entrance to the terrace and bar
10. Stairway
11. 1000-foot cinder track
12. Ramp connecting the health service (17th floor) with the terrace and the day nursery
13. Day nursery
14. Kindergarten
15. Swimming pool
16. Balcony
17. Windbreaker (open-air theater)

The Marseilles Apartment Block (Unité d'Habitation), 1945-1952.
Plan of the Terrace-Roof.
Cross-Section: Two two-story flats interlock in such a way that there is room between them on the middle floor for an interior street (R).

The cross-section shows clearly the internal arrangement of the Housing Unit (Unité d'Habitation). All the apartments are oriented to both east and west, all are disposed on two levels and have a living room with double floor height. They are connected by an internal street which, at every second level, runs over the whole length of the building: the apartment is entered either at the level of the living room (upper type of flat) or at the level of the loggia (lower type of flat). The number of floor stops thus being limited to eight, the elevator service is accelerated and made more economical. The Housing Unit is completed by a shopping center on the sixth and seventh levels (realized only in Marseilles).

Cross-Section of the Apartment Block showing the course of the sun in summer and winter.

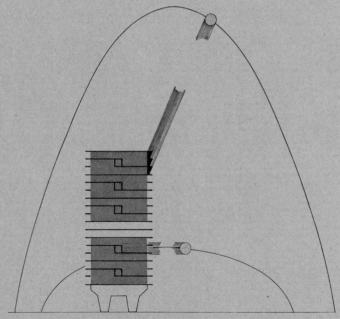

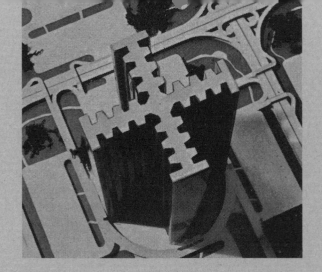

From about 1914 to 1922, from Futurism (Sant'Elia) to Expressionism (Bruno Taut, Scharoun) and Constructivism (Tatlin, Lissitzky, Gabo), the skyscraper was one of the main themes of the neo-romantic approach to the big city: we find it in the "cathedral of Socialism," the woodcut by Feininger illustrating the first Bauhaus manifesto; also in the—very modest—Einstein Tower of Mendelsohn and in certain projects by Mies van der Rohe. But in 1924 the competition for the Chicago Tribune building led a certain number of European architects to take a less purely poetical view of the skyscraper and to pass on from the free sketch to the analysis of a precise program and actual building conditions. In France, Perret had already systematically studied the possibility of erecting high-rise buildings with a reinforced concrete framework (and not, as in the United States, with a metal skeleton). But Perret too, like many others addicted to crystal-gazing, went so far, in an interview, as to evoke a Utopian vision of "tower-cities."

Beginning with his Contemporary City of 1922, Le Corbusier made ample allowance for skyscrapers in his town-planning projects. Not that he attached any symbolic or monumental value to them. Indeed, going against the current fashion, he refused to emphasize their verticality and rather oddly described his first skyscrapers, built on a cruciform plan, as "horizontal skyscrapers." By that he meant that, the length of the arms of the cross being proportioned to the height of the edifice, the horizontal formed by the roof terraces gives the skyline of a series of skyscrapers that impeccable straightness which best suits the Business Center.

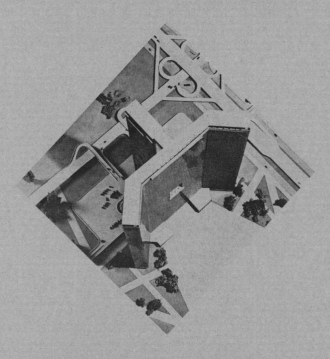

Cruciform Skyscraper, 1925.
Designed for the Voisin Plan of Paris.

Cartesian Skyscraper, 1930.

Star-Shaped Skyscraper, 1933.
Designed for Algiers.

For the skyscraper is an "instrument" to which Le Corbusier, in his conception of the city, assigned a precise place and function. A small number of super-skyscrapers would house the whole of that Business Center which formed the core of what he later called la métropole des échanges, the change-over city (that is, a metropolis with diverse functions). This concentration permitted the creation around them of the Green City: "Right in the business center, where sky-scrapers may be erected, the city still remains green and trees reign supreme; men, in the shelter of them, live under the aegis of proportion: the man-nature relationship is re-established." But, owing to the inflow and outflow of the thousands of people working in each skyscraper, this concentration raises acute traffic problems. Accordingly, in the Voisin Plan which he drew up in 1925 for a proposed reconstruction of the center of Paris, the office skyscraper has as its indispensable complement a whole system of traffic arteries. In thus treating the skyscraper not as an isolated piece of architecture but, like the multistory villas, as an integrated urban unit, Le Corbusier made it one of the determinant elements of the "order of size" which he considered essential for the large modern city.

Lozenge-Shaped Skyscraper designed for Algiers, 1938. Model and floor plan.

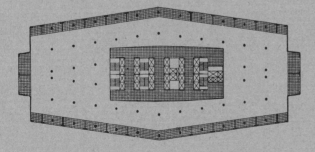

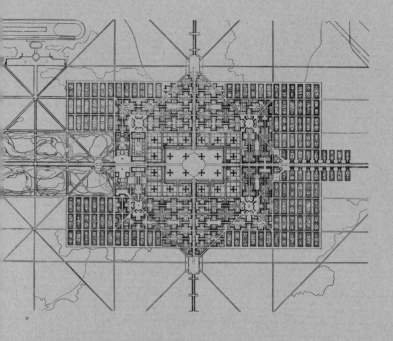

"A Contemporary City of Three Million Inhabitants."
Study presented at the Salon d'Automne, Paris, 1922.

In the Contemporary City planned by Le Corbusier in 1922, the business center was entirely surrounded by a residential district composed of apartment blocks laid out on an indented plan, the blocks being alternately set back and projected forward. Industry was relegated to the periphery. The two main traffic arteries intersected at right angles in the center of the city. In the Radiant City, this concentric layout was abandoned in favor of a linear pattern: "Remember," noted Le Corbusier, "that organic life, in the course of the evolution of species, leaves the primary stage of the concentric cell to follow an axis, to take a direction, to fix a goal for itself." The "biological development" of the city can take place freely on either side of this axis, by the lateral extension of each of the zones which make up the city and which are aligned on the axis that gives the city its orientation. "The principle is clear: housing is the basic element. The other elements, work and recreation, must be arranged so as to avoid sterile journeys."
The indented apartment blocks, while occupying only a small proportion of the ground (12%), should permit a very high density of population (about 1000 inhabitants for every 2 1/2 acres).

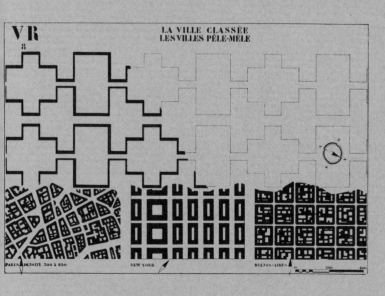

"Ordered city, pell-mell cities."
Diagram of the indented apartment blocks of the Radiant City as compared with street patterns of Paris,
New York, and Buenos Aires drawn on the same scale.
Study presented at the Brussels congress of CIAM, 1930.

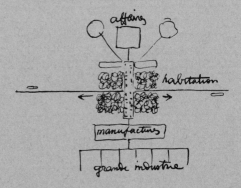

Sketch of the Radiant City.

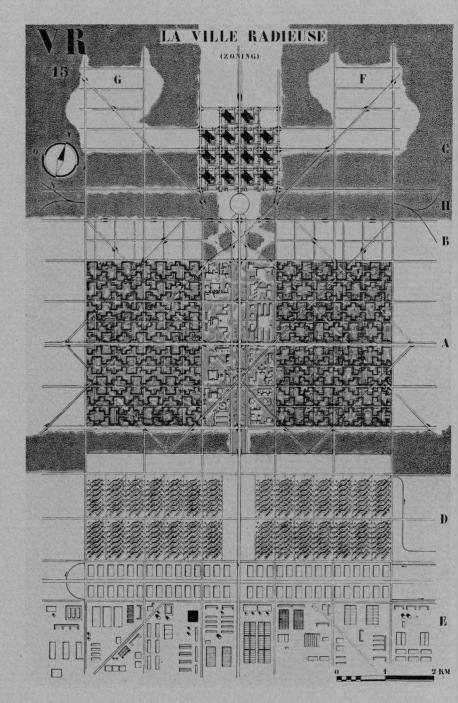

Zoning of the Radiant City.
Study presented at the Brussels congress
of CIAM, 1930.

A. *Housing*
B. *Hotels and embassies*
C. *Business center*
D. *Factories and warehouses*
E. *Heavy industry*
F. *and G. Satellite towns (e.g. seat of*
government, center of social studies, etc.)

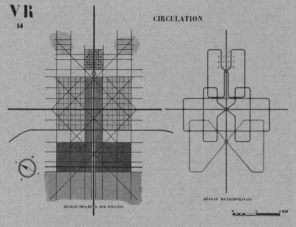

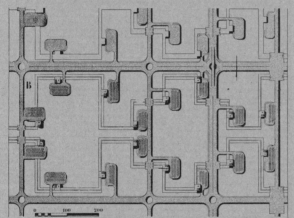

The idea of a "river system" of "classified traffic," able to move in a coordinated and continuous flow, represents one of the most important aspects, for the future of town-planning, of the Radiant City project presented by Le Corbusier at the CIAM congress in Brussels. Motor traffic, operating on two levels according to speed, is distributed over a much more efficient network of highways, and this is directly connected with the vertical elevator traffic of the apartment blocks; pedestrian traffic is wholly independent of it. The subway system, completing the network of surface traffic, is also designed to facilitate and accelerate the movement of passengers.

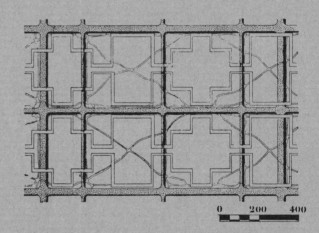

Traffic in the Radiant City (CIAM, Brussels, 1930):
Roads and carports (parking areas) serving the indented apartment blocks. Automobile and pedestrian traffic.
Independence of pedestrian traffic in relation to automobile traffic and to the position of the apartment blocks.

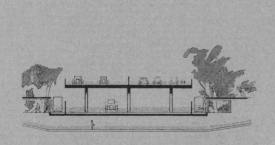

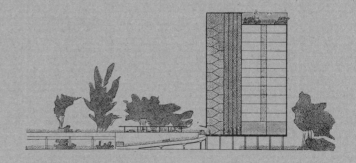

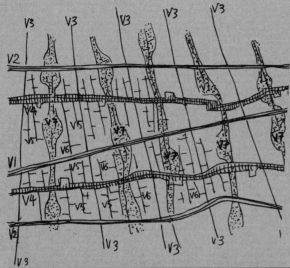

The Road Network of the 7 V's, 1945.

V 1: interurban motorway
V 2: main axis of urban traffic
V 3: interurban network of motor traffic
V 4: commercial street within the city sectors
V 5 and V 6: streets serving the houses
V 7: pedestrian walk

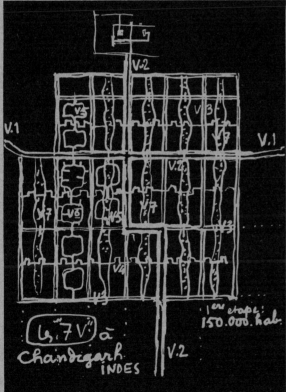

Fifteen years later Le Corbusier devised what he called the system of the 7 V's (V = voie, road). This was an even more strict and efficient classification of traffic, with a view to ensuring its continuous flow. The 7 V system was applied in full at Chandigarh. Starting with the very large interurban artery V1, it ends with the fine capillary network of V7 in the green belt. "V7," wrote Le Corbusier, "is a green linear zone which irrigates the different sectors of the city... These large green belts contain the schools, the playgrounds, etc. They pass from one sector to another by the same outlets as the V5 roads." The key elements are V3, which delimits the sectors, and V4. To the latter Le Corbusier attached special importance: "V4 channels off the city traffic from points of intense activity. V4 is the road that gives its peculiar character to each sector of the city. Therefore each V4 will be different from the others and equipped with specific characteristics, for it is indispensable to create an urban setting of great variety and to provide the inhabitants with the elements of classification. It is V4 that will fulfill the traditional social functions of the street."

Application of the 7 V System at Chandigarh, 1951.

169

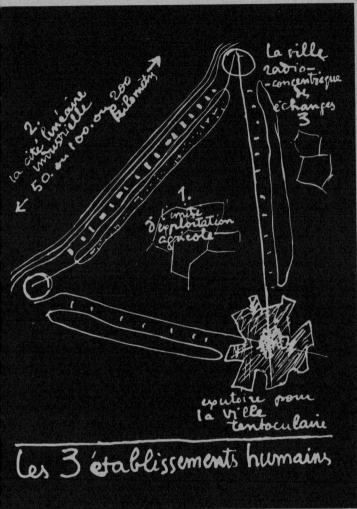

The Radiant City was polyvalent: it was a center combining business, administration (even government), and production. The separation he later made between the "radio-concentric change-over metropolis" and the "linear industrial city" might be interpreted as a strict application of the principle of zoning laid down in the Athens Charter. It seems more reasonable, however, to regard this separation as an effort to adapt the urban tools to the layout of the traffic network, in which Le Corbusier had now come to see the basic instrument of the "occupation of the territory." With the linear industrial city, the secondary function, hitherto somewhat neglected, found a form well suited to its peculiar needs: "The linear industrial city is proportioned in accordance with the human scale and the course of the sun. It is the great town-planning creation of modern times. The countryside has become machine-minded too and offers up its vast green and sown expanses between the linear cities irrigating the territory." The ASCORAL map, drawn up during the Second World War, extrapolated the network of linear industrial cities destined to be woven over the Eurasian continent from the Atlantic to China: "The subject was anathema and dangerous in that year 1943. Today the gun frontiers are breaking down, the economic zones stand out naturally, and the highroads of the linear cities will go from the Atlantic to China. An eternal and fateful process: already, in the early days of human society, and with no other vehicle but the striding of men, these same highroads were travelled over. This justifies us in setting down this term: 'End of a World': the three human establishments."

"The Three Human Establishments," 1945:

1. The Farm Unit
2. The Linear Industrial City
3. The Radio-Concentric Change-Over City

The Natural Occupation of the Territory.
ASCORAL Map of Europe, 1943.

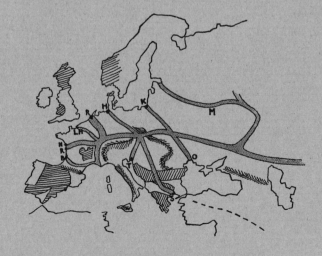

By then, the inadequate nature of any research merely confined to the city as such had become self-evident; what now needed defining and, once again, "classifying" was nothing less than the complete set of relations existing inside the "territory" (for Le Corbusier this was synonymous with the Continent). The very notion of town-planning was by now outmoded, the emphasis was all on traffic and circulation (the Four Routes, the 7 Vs).

And so, through forty years, Le Corbusier treated the numerous cities for which he drew up reconstruction projects always according to the same principles. Neither the intervening evolution nor the historical diversity of the concrete situations he had to face, nor yet the technical complexity of that singular domain that town-planning increasingly became—nothing, during those forty years, was apparently able to undermine the convictions he had already sketched in broad outline as far back as 1922-1925. This unwavering persistence is doubtless explained, and perhaps even justified, by the insurmountable opposition evinced by authorities everywhere—with the one exception of Nehru's India—to the application of two principles which, in Le Corbusier's eyes, represented the *sine qua non* of all town-planning: the acceptance of the "order of size," answering to the civilization of the largest number, and the concerted implementation of the entire set of "instruments of urban renovation." Did this vain and tragic struggle bring on a form of sclerosis, preventing Le Corbusier from proceeding to the indispensable revision of a system that for him had meanwhile become a personal one of self-defense? The answer given to this question depends too directly on the value one attaches to the component ideas of that system to provide much clarification.

Who was Le Corbusier the town-planner? A "terrible oversimplifier," the long-delayed heir, already outmoded, of the eighteenth and nineteenth century Utopians, indifferent to the real man and recognizing only man-machine? Or an intuitive genius blazing a princely trail, so far ahead of his time that the specialists with their analyses have still not caught up with him? Was he the "Procrustean aesthete" alleged by Lewis Mumford, his bitterest detractor? Or was he, as he would have wished to be, the liberator of a humanity that had become the master of technology and was no longer its slave?

The debate centers less on the composition of the tools proposed (the argument here revolved around the Housing Unit) than on the very idea of grouping the different functions of the city into standardized architectural units, isolated and distributed according to an apparently uniform system of zoning. To treat the city as the arithmetical sum of a few elementary and stable functions would seem to be an arbitrary oversimplification; for does not the life of the city consist in a constant challenge to the equilibrium of multiple functions which are themselves continually evolving? The establishment of relations between functions varies for each social group, each family, each individual; are standard architectural instruments capable of assuming this shifting multiplicity of functions and of adapting themselves to their continual transformations? Sociology suggests that the modern city forms a nontypified tissue of cells, each different and each having its specific function; can this functional continuity of the urban tissue, expressed in its visual continuity, be maintained within a structure based on the purely mechanical articulation of organs separated from one another? Is the freeing of the ground obtained by vertical concentration really a functional liberation also? Does not the "death of the street" signify rather the death of the city? Finally, however radical the transformations effected in the structure of the city by industrial civilization, does not the city, each city in particular, find its essential definition in the continuity of an original historical development? Le Corbusier refused to decongest the old city by creating satellite cities, and demanded that the transformation be effected on the spot; but in so doing, did he not cut off the city from its roots and project it into what was no more than the illusion of a future? Did he not aim, like all Utopians, to wrench the city from its historical bed?

Despite an occasional tribute to Fourier and his phalanstery, Le Corbusier always strenuously denied any Utopian intentions. From the time of his book *Urbanisme*, for instance, he took up a clear stand against the "tower-cities" of Perret, claiming that the extrapolation of the principle of exploiting three dimensions "was not realistic." In proposing the complete renewal of urban tools and techniques, he intended rather to prove his historical realism, to place himself in the very stream of history. Inasmuch as every age had created the tools best suited to its way of life, it would be flying in the face of history to refuse the society of the machine age the right to do the same. But this society itself was not free to shift the center of gravity of the "change-over cities": the localization of that center was linked too directly with the network of pathways and relations, near and far, which had their foundation in geography and their evolution in history. So many values, material and immaterial, had been invested in it that any shift would prove fatal to the process of continuity, though this process did not exclude the mutations to which the renewal of the tools must correspond. Le Corbusier's respect for historical continuity thus moved him at once to reject any suggestion of tampering with the axis of Paris, and at the same time to propose that, within the existing urban fabric, the business center and the high-speed traffic arteries feeding it be shifted slightly to the north, it being essential at all costs to conserve the architectural integrity of such a historic center.

That sense of history which enabled Le Corbusier to grasp the supreme vocation of the city—not infrequently in contradiction to the analysis of the specialist—was one essential component of his activity as a town-planner. In Chandigarh, for instance, he at once realized and stressed the symbolic function of a city which the Oxford team before him had only treated from the residential aspect. In Venice, contrary to general expectation, he did not propose some monumental composition with a new version of the Procuratie; instead, his hospital project was based on the same idea as his plan for the renewal of Ilôt No. 6 in Paris: the complete—and generalizable—renewal of the urban equipment (built-up masses and traffic masses) was here contemplated without in any way threatening the living continuity of the fabric. If Le Corbusier refused to shift the center of gravity of historic cities, this was because he realized that their fate was bound up with the streets which were but an extension, within their precincts, of the network of roads linking them with the world, and which were a part of them, in the words of one geographer, "far more substantially than the masses of stones that enclose them." The street for him was so much a physical reality, neither linear nor abstract, but three-dimensional, that he wrote, for instance, in 1930: "The town councillors

of the machine age have not yet managed to grasp the fact that the street is not a crust laid on the earth's surface but a *building in length*, an edifice, a *container*, and not an outer skin." That the one-tier web of old-time streets, derived from the "donkey path," must henceforth be replaced by a "classified" system according to the "contents," and formed of several superimposed networks; that this classification of the means of circulation constitutes the precondition of any regeneration of the street, and hence of the town—all this is accepted almost unanimously today. How Le Corbusier understood this classification is best shown in the Chandigarh project. Articulated about the counterpoint of the rectilinear "V 3s" of high-speed automobile approach roads dividing off sectors of 800 by 1200 meters, and pathways for pedestrians, shops, and leisure pursuits interlinking these sectors, he envisaged a network sufficiently loose-knit to enable all the functions— except those of government—to be shifted from sector to sector and the pathways to be reorganized in accordance with future needs. Though apparently more rigid than the earlier project drawn up by town-planners inspired by the works of Clarence Stein, Le Corbusier's project was in fact infinitely more flexible, and would—had the authorities of the Punjab capital only been willing to exploit the possibilities it offered—have given rise to a subtly differentiated and richly sinewed urban network.

However, the most violent argument centered, and still centers, on what Le Corbusier himself presented as the essential contribution of "liberating technics": the freeing of the greater part of the ground by concentrating the constructed masses in terms of height. It is here that we witness the confrontation of two ideas, one might even say two myths: that of the city and that of nature. The combination of the two proposed by Le Corbusier, when he claimed to establish the "conditions of nature" in the very heart of the city, struck both urbanists and naturists as nonsensical and Utopian. While the former held out for the continuity of the built-up area, the latter advocated the retention of the individual dwelling; while the former opted for interpenetration, the latter wanted deconcentration of the functions; both agreed in arguing against the idea of the Radiant City, citing in illustration the human breakdown observed in most of the allotments of "aerated" dwellings constructed since the last war.

At this point, it is as well to emphasize that, forty years after the elaboration of the Radiant City, one still cannot fairly argue for it or against it on the basis of any concrete realization of the ideas it contained. In particular, none of the dormitory-cities, in which the application of the Athens Charter was reduced to a simple exercise in hygiene, fulfilled the conditions of the Radiant City as defined by Le Corbusier. In any case, this is not the place to deal in detail with an argument which, in addition to infinitely complex matters of fact, introduces widely opposing ideological and emotional points of view. We can at best hope to show how the great themes of Le Corbusier's town-planning projects followed that same line of thought which gave birth to his architectural schemes, how the organization of architectural space in his hands prepared the way and finally made way for the organization of urban space, and even social space in general.

Now, as a town-planner, Le Corbusier at first appears to be just as much the plastic artist as he was when, in painting, he organized the surface of a picture or, in architecture, he regulated the "play of forms in light." A plastic artist, creating a visual order of things that should not only satisfy man's reason but also touch his heart: in Le Corbusier's eyes, just as architecture was something more than mere construction, so town-planning had more to it than the discharge of a certain number of functions, embracing also of necessity what Sitte in his old age termed the "art of building towns," the setting out and scaling of solid masses and voids. "The outside is always an inside." A town, however functional it may be, is not a plan, but a site, a landscape. Moreover, "town-planning is a science in three dimensions indissolubly interlinked... everything which affects the surface can exist only as a function of the height. Herein lies the key to every solution." One of the corollaries of this fundamental postulate of spatial urbanism is that the quality of all town-planning is closely dependent on the quality and more especially the scale of the architecture in which it is embodied. The great buildings on which Le Corbusier's town-planning projects are articulated—however few in number their types—are themselves articulated with one another and with the spaces they punctuate in such a way as to provide the spectator, as he goes along, with sites that are highly characterized and whose aspect is constantly being renewed. From the regulatory pattern governing the layout of the World City to the grid devised for imbricating the indented housing blocks of the Radiant City, Le Corbusier multiplied those devices which could be relied upon to provide the appearance of the town with both unity and—despite the repetition of the same basic elements—diversity, in line with the maxim of the Abbé Laugier which he cited on more than one occasion: "Chaos, confusion in the whole, uniformity in the detail." It is not hard to imagine the wealth of visual itineraries afforded by the play of the masses found in the plans destined for, say, Antwerp, Bogotá, or Saint-Dié.

For Le Corbusier, the advance from the "pell-mell city" to the "ordered city," from the "choked-up city" to the open city, became the only method that would restore to urban life that unity of scale whose absence rendered the modern megalopolis so oppressive. The question whether the order of size resulting from this mutation could be adapted to the human scale, or whether the increasingly huge dimensions of intra-urban spaces did not threaten to create a new feeling of alienation in the modern city-dweller—this problem caused Le Corbusier, by his own admission, much doubt and anguish: "In providing for vast empty spaces in this imaginary city, dominated everywhere by the overspreading sky, I was very much afraid that these empty spaces might be 'dead,' that boredom might reign and panic seize the people living there." The masterly harmony of mathematical ratios balancing the constructed masses against the free spaces was no adequate guarantee against the danger of alienation that might be produced by the unfamiliar dimensions of the new urban site. "Gigantomachy?" questioned Le Corbusier, referring to the skyscrapers of the Radiant City, and gave his own answer: "No. The miracle of trees and parks restores the human scale."

The large-scale introduction of trees into the heart of the city was thus the result, not of some rather naïve faith in the magic power of its verdure, some Rousseauesque romanticism in favor of natural disorder in opposition to the abstract geometry of man-made schemes. In the tree, Le Corbusier saw not only the mainstay of those "conditions of nature" (sun, space, greenery) that were for him the dispensers of the "essential joys" of life; the tree also provided the key value in the scale which was to help re-establish a visual and dimensional continuity between man—a natural, biological invariable—and the anti-natural medium of the town. Without reconstituting the "corridor-street," which breaks up space, the tree did recreate that intermediary level of 25 to 40 feet which, in traditional towns with their continuous individual dwellings, served as a visual base for the major piece of architecture, in the shape of the church or the mosque. It was for the same reason that Le Corbusier limited the height of his Housing Units to eight double stories, his idea being that, from the top floor, visual contact could still be maintained with the tree, which in turn represented a yardstick indicating the scale of the neighboring site. Over and above this height, that scale would no longer be perceptible. It was not only for the allegedly refreshing effect of its mass of foliage—which in any case lasted for barely six months in the year—that the tree occupied such an important place in Le Corbusier's town-planning projects, but above all because it seemed to him to be the biologically organized form best suited to providing man with the landmark he needed to find his bearings in the totally new "order of size" of machine civilization and its equipment. In the collective living-machine that the city ultimately was, the tree also became an organ no less essential than those other organs of which the "urban equipment" was composed. It was through the tree that the city's anti-natural order of size was linked up with the biological order of the natural world.

This singular departure, often misunderstood, thus brings to light one of the essential presuppositions of Le Corbusier's architectural and urbanist thought:

namely, his insistence on the need to link every organized form to the human scale, the tree, as a natural unit of measure, serving simply to connect man with the scale of the site. For Le Corbusier, the organization of space, in both architecture and town-planning, was never equivalent to a problem of composing with masses, but consisted in the last resort in working out a system of measurements which would guarantee to man the complete functional and visual control of his environment. For him, every living form, whether natural or constructed, was ultimately organization ("Architecture is organization," he told a gathering of would-be architects in 1938. "You are organizers, not drawing-board artists."); and this organization could only be translated by numbers. Whether Le Corbusier, pencil in hand, tried to grasp the law of organization of a plant or a sea-shell, or to work out the best possible articulation of the various organs of the city, the margins of his sketches nearly always ended up littered with figures, numerical ratios. Seeing was for him synonymous with measuring. In the extremely wide sense in which he understood the two notions, biology and mathematics seemed to him to form one organic whole. This being so, the whole problem of contemporary town-planning consisted, in his view, in defining the intermediate values of a scale capable of establishing a ratio at once viable and realizable, and so necessarily flexible, between the permanent dimensions of man and a universe—the world of urbanism—lacking all measure in the sense that it was no longer based on any assured dimensional constant. The equation plasticity = biology = mathematics emerges as at once the prime postulate of all Le Corbusier's work and thought, whether in painting, architecture, or town-planning.

Town-Planning Sketches:
"Beauty, Homeland, Protection of the Homeland?
The protectors of the homeland are those who create it."

Town-Planning Sketches:
"Beauty, Homeland, Protection of the Homeland?
The protectors of the homeland are those who create it."

"At Rio de Janeiro, a city which seems radiantly to defy all human collaboration with its universally recognized beauty, a violent desire, perhaps a wild desire, comes over you to attempt here again a human adventure—the desire to engage in a duel, a contest of 'human affirmation' against or with 'nature's presence'." An elevated motorway winds in and out between bays and peaks and sends out tentacles towards the valleys and the harbor, where it ends on the roofs of the commercial office buildings, here designated as "seascrapers." Under the motorway, following the lie of the land, extends a continuous band of gigantic apartment blocks. The solution is revolutionary, but the reference once again is twofold: contemporary (the trial speedway on the roof of the Fiat plant) and classical (the Roman aqueduct). *"This aqueduct, outside the scale of the houses, will destroy the site? No, it won't! The aqueduct has made the site."* And his pencil confirmed this: *"At sea off Rio, I took up my sketchbook: I drew the mountains and, between the mountains, the future motorway and the great architectural belt that carries it: and the peaks... were enhanced by this impeccable horizontal. The passing liners, those magnificent, moving buildings of modern times, found yonder, hanging in space over the city, a response, an echo, a reply. The whole site began speaking, on sea, on land, and in the air: it spoke architecture. This discourse was a poem of human geometry and of immense natural fantasy. The eye saw something, it saw two things: nature and the product of man's handiwork. The presence of the city was announced by a line which, by itself, is capable of singing with the vehement whimsy of the mountains: the horizontal line."*

Neither the vertical garden-city nor the commercial skyscraper nor the traffic network took an immutable form. All were instruments, variously fashioned, whose sole purpose was to permit the application of the fundamental principle of the new town-planning: the creation of space. Their forms had accordingly to be adapted to the geography of the places where they were installed. The Rio sketches and the plans for Algiers are a spectacular illustration not only of the plasticity of these "instruments" but of Le Corbusier's wonderful knack of scaling his architectural landscapes even to the most cramped of natural sites.

The site of Algiers presented a further difficulty: the presence of the old town, the Kasbah, which it was important to regenerate and emphasize. Here the coastal strip is so narrow that space could only be created by means of "artificial plots": that meant building upwards, while at the same time laying stress on the horizontal line, the only line compatible with the movement of the site. Finally, it was necessary to establish quick and easy connections with the plateau, at an altitude of 500 feet, the only available reserve of space, in a grandiose and wholesome site. As at Rio, Le Corbusier provided for an elevated motorway running parallel to the shore line, with apartment blocks beneath it capable of housing 180,000 people. Another raised motorway would lead by an overpass directly from the plateau to the top of the "seascrapers" in the business district, skirting the historic Kasbah on the west and leaving it intact. On the plateau itself, apartment blocks on the indented pattern, of gigantic size (inner enclosure of 4,000 by 2,600 feet), would form "the tiara on the head of Algiers." Their curving forms answer to the same conception which, at Ronchamp, Le Corbusier described as "landscape acoustics": "They respond to a call from the landscape, a creative event of a plastic order: the response to the horizons carries further; the response to the winds and sun is truer. Actually, a lyrical event, which counts to an eminent degree, and which crowns a rational process."

Town-Planning Scheme for Algiers (Project A), 1930.
Viaduct apartment block along the shore and intended apartment block of Fort-l'Empereur connected by an overpass with the "seascrapers" of the business center.

Town-Planning Study for Rio de Janeiro, 1936.
Project for a motorway running on top of a continuous band of apartment blocks. Pen drawing.

Le Corbusier's town-planning proposals for Paris are marked by a dual and unvarying refusal: on the one hand, he refused to decentralize, to transfer anything into the suburbs, to break up the "business center"; on the other, he rejected the notorious idea of a "triumphal axis" prolonging the Champs-Elysées on the west and, on the east, running into the "dead-end of the Concorde." In his Voisin Plans of 1922 and 1925, Le Corbusier proposed to clear away the crowded slum quarters stretching southward from the heights of Montmartre and the Buttes-Chaumont, and to establish the business center there. In his final project the number of skyscrapers was reduced to four: "In that plain, cleared of meaningless buildings, which extends in the direction of Saint-Denis, far from the mementoes of the past standing on the banks of the river, four great architectural events will occupy a broad space, to the glory of a civilization which, far from abdicating, has again marked out for itself a line of conduct." As for traffic, Le Corbusier articulated it on crisscrossing axes, the most important of which in his eyes was the east-west axis, which would enable him to restore the unity of a city divided into two halves, each foreign to the other, by the segregationist planning of Haussmann. This main east-west axis passed to the north of the historic zone, which could thus be fully revalorized by shunting transit traffic away from it. According to the project presented by Le Corbusier in 1932 with a view to the Paris World's Fair of 1937, it was along this axis, beginning on the east, that his Radiant City would be built in successive stages, following the model worked out for the renovation of the Paris slum district known as Ilôt No. 6.

Above: Urban Project for Paris.
Model of the Voisin Plan showing
a projected business center opposite the Cité.
Model exhibited in the Pavillon de L'Esprit Nouveau
at the Exhibition of Decorative Arts, Paris, 1925.

Below: Urban Project for Paris.
Photomontage showing the reorganization
of the district north of the Ile de la Cité.
Project exhibited at the Paris World's Fair, 1937.

Urban Project for Paris.
Creation of a business center between the Châtelet
and the heights of Montmartre and Les Buttes-Chaumont.
Pen drawing, 1945. (Further development of the Voisin
Plan)

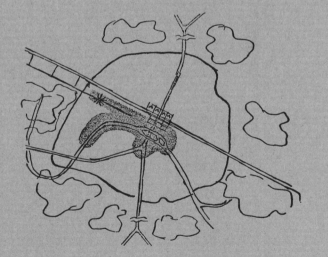

Plan for Paris, 1937.
The main east-west axis, showing projected connections
with suburban trunk roads.

Sketch for the Reconstruction of Saint-Dié (Vosges), eastern France. Pen drawing made on the spot by Le Corbusier, 1945 or 1946.

The historic center of Saint-Dié was completely destroyed in the Second World War. The plan which Le Corbusier was invited to submit for its reconstruction was very nearly carried into effect, but local politics intervened and in the end, unfortunately, it was rejected. His project was a particularly interesting one. In three respects it proposed revolutionary solutions. First of all, it applied to the small town the formula of the Housing Unit (Unité d'Habitation). Next, the social and civic center, composed of a series of buildings of varying shapes and sizes offering ever-changing vistas, brought together the "organs" of collective life (town hall, civic auditorium, theater, museum, department store)

and treated them as "architectural events" of breathtaking beauty, their volumes being carefully designed to harmonize with the remaining buildings of the old town and with the configuration and skyline of the surrounding mountains. Finally, a linear industrial city would have been built, its plants, warehouses, and public utility installations standing apart from the civic center but in proximity to the main lines of communication (highways, railroads, river). The whole plan was carefully drawn to the "scale of the man on foot" and everything was so calculated that the distance between a man's home and his place of work would never be more than he could walk in a quarter of an hour.

Model of the Projected Reconstruction of Saint-Dié, 1945.

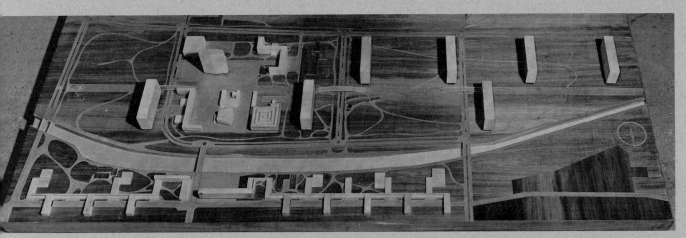

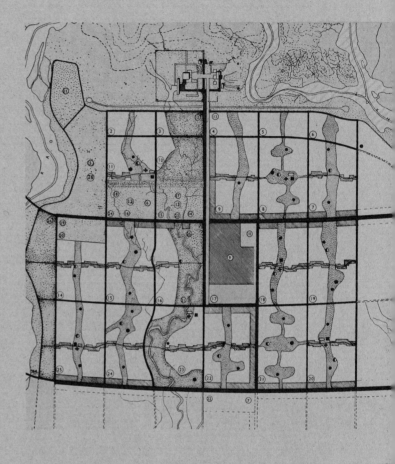

Master Plan for Chandigarh (Punjab), India.
Left: Plan proposed by Albert Mayer, 1950.
Right: Definitive plan drawn up by Le Corbusier, 1951.

At Chandigarh, it was Le Corbusier's task to build the Capitol (*cf. pp. 185-192*) and to lay out the plan of the city. This plan resembles that of the Radiant City not only in its general arrangement but in certain particular features: the off-center position of the governmental complex, the checker-pattern division into sectors (whose size was increased to 4,000 by 2,600 feet) and the classified traffic system. But its true significance can be seen only by relating it to the special requirements which the town-planner had to meet at Chandigarh, and by comparing it with the initial project drawn up by the firm of Albert Mayer. Apart from its perfected system of circulation (designed, moreover, to cope with a volume of traffic which Chandigarh is far from having attained), Le Corbusier's plan is essentially characterized by his outright rejection of the garden-city solution and by his emphasis, in the geometric rigor of its articulation, on the distinctively political vocation of Chandigarh. Nowhere else does one see more clearly the moral significance which Le Corbusier attached to the rejection of the "donkey path" which, even more than in Europe, traced out the cities of India; nowhere else in his work did this rejection have a comparable repercussion. India had already had, in New Delhi, a city laid out on geometric lines, but there it had been imposed from outside by a colonial power. At Chandigarh, this geometric order appears as the expression of India's own will to action in the modern world, and one can hardly overestimate the psychological value of this dramatic break with the traditional order, or disorder, of the Indian city. The will to renewal of the promoters of the project did not, however, go beyond this symbolic affirmation. While their conservatism did not press too heavily on the conception of the city plan as a whole, it did, on the other hand, check the development of the architectural fabric that had to be fitted into that plan. The latter, however, is flexible enough to adapt itself to any changes liable to take place in the sociological structure of the city.

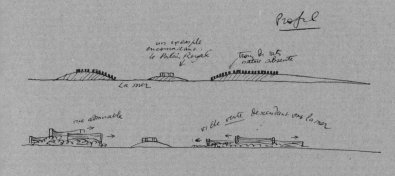

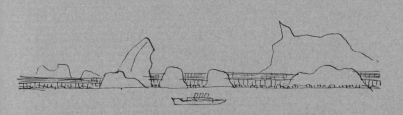

Town-Planning Sketches.
"This for Algiers

and that for Stockholm

For Rio de Janeiro...
And for Paris and Antwerp,

the Green City and its essential joys."

In Algiers, Stockholm, Rio, Paris, Antwerp, Buenos Aires, Saint-Dié, Bogotá, La Rochelle, Geneva, and Berlin, the town-planning schemes drawn up by Le Corbusier were rejected out of hand as fanciful and inhuman. Leaving Algiers on July 22, 1934, after three successive projects of his had been rejected, Le Corbusier noted: "They are driving me away. They have closed the doors on me. I go, and I feel this profoundly: I'm right, I'm right, I'm right... It is a bitter sorrow to see men devoted to their city stubbornly deny it the smile of art and the attitude of grandeur."

In the century of the urban explosion, the only contemporary who had not only an innate sense of the grandeur of the new civilization but a respect for the "historical biology" of the city was allowed to put his ideas into practice only once—in the Punjab. "The protectors of the homeland," he wrote one day, referring to the "Heimatschutz" leagues in Germany which, at the Weissenhof exhibition in 1927, had first accused him of "Kulturbolschewismus," "the protectors of the homeland are those who create it."

Nehru's India, alone among the nations, took him at his word and acted on it.

Masterpieces in profusion bear witness to the perfect manner in which Le Corbusier's methodology always proved adequate to his creative endeavor both as plastic artist and especially as architect. By contrast, in the field of town-planning, in which he left us only theoretical investigations and projects which did not advance beyond the stage of studies of principle, the polemical fashion in which he almost invariably presented his views sometimes left the impression that this equation was too narrow a base on which to erect a framework of social life.

Of all Le Corbusier's proposals, it is doubtless in relation to the Radiant City that we find the most flagrant expression of that ambiguity regarding the true sense of his work engendered by the obstinacy with which he presented and defended, as being an intellectual construction deriving from pure logic, what was in fact the fruit of an infinitely more complex creative process. As in the concept of the living-machines, many very different motivations were here at work in preparing, not the establishment of some deductive synthesis, but the opening-up of a vision. Though not that of an aesthete, this vision was none the less aesthetic in nature: the vision of a social space, the harmonious occupation of which would be ensured by the play of a small number of organs and standards, at once free and strictly regulated, inside it. Having reinvented architectural space, as Cézanne had reinvented pictorial space, on the basis of its most elementary data; having at the same time found, in the analogy of the machine, a formula which seemed to him to translate, in terms provocative enough to effect a breakthrough, a creative undertaking in which the reasons of the heart—what he himself described as *la passion*— played (fortunately) as decisive a part as pure reason;

moving subsequently, by a perfectly legitimate transition, on to the plane of social space, Le Corbusier maintained and even reinforced the machine analogy as a method of exposition, heedless of the dangers it involved at this level. Upon that flexible and sensitive logic, that spirit of finesse to which each of his architectural creations bore witness, that analogy in fact superimposed another logic—a logic quite uncompromising in its demonstrations—which lent to what was in fact the fruit of free and open intuition the disagreeably didactic trappings of a closed system. The "design" here betrayed the motive purpose; the spirit of geometry appeared, unreservedly and uninhibitedly, to have gained the day.

Profile of the Capitol at Chandigarh (above).
Model (below) made on the spot by Rattan Singh, showing the position of the Secretariat, the Assembly Hall, the Governor's Palace and the Palace of Justice (Law Courts).

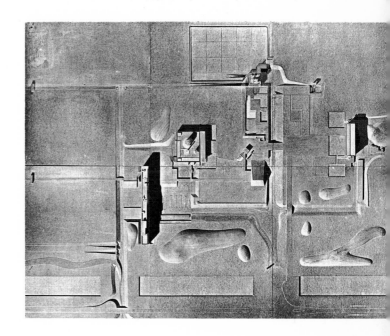

Chandigarh: The Secretariat (left) and the Assembly Hall (right) seen from the main entrance of the Palace of Justice.

"Signify by art the epic conquest of the New Age." In 1951, at Chandigarh, the new capital of the Punjab, the problem was very similar to what it had been in Moscow twenty years earlier. But in newly independent India, poverty-stricken, economically and socially backward, the idiom employed could not be the same. While in the Palace of the Soviets he had emphatically made the most of technics and machine forms, at Chandigarh, by the force of circumstances, he worked on simpler, almost primitive lines, yet, as always, with a fresh, wholly modern approach: while admirably adapted to the Indian situation, the Chandigarh idiom is in tune with the times, just as that of the Palace of the Soviets had been.

Again the basic reference was the Campo Santo in Pisa, although the limited means at his disposal ruled out any high-rise buildings. The method, as usual, consisted in bringing together "organs defined independently of each other," the civic center designed for Saint-Dié representing the preparatory stage. The plan was on an epic scale: the esplanade, bordered on east and west by the strict prisms of the Palace of Justice and the Secretariat, measures 400 by 800 meters, with the animated silhouettes of the Assembly Hall and the Governor's Palace (not built) standing out against the Himalayas. On either side, a recreation park and an artificial lake bordered by a promenade provide restful horizontal surfaces in harmony with the overall plan.

Chandigarh: West Front of the Secretariat, 1958.

Chandigarh: The Palace of Justice seen from the Assembly Hall, 1956.

While everything is on a large scale, nothing is disproportionate. For in the final reckoning the scale is determined neither by the site nor by a political ideal, but everywhere and always by man, and by man at his humblest. Of the project for the Governor's Palace, Le Corbusier wrote: "In the course of the three years 1951-1953, the project development took shape. 1954: crisis! The costs are infinitely too high! What happened? The plans having been accepted, they were revised in respect to the general heights and sizes of the various parts... and since it was for the Governor they had slipped in on the side the largest dimensions of the Modulor. The volume proved to be double that of the original project! And the scale of the Palace grew enormous! They had designed for the scale of giants! All was reconsidered. The choice of sufficiently low dimensions of the Modulor cut the cubage of the building in half and restored it to the human scale. The final working drawings demonstrate that we have thus placed the Governor in a man's house."

It is here that the comparison, so tempting and so often attempted, between the Capitol of Chandigarh and Michelangelo's redesigned Capitol in Rome breaks down. Le Corbusier never built for princes or supermen, nor for "communists, capitalists, MRP's or XYZ's"; he built for men, whose measure he tried to take as exactly and universally as possible. For if man was not for him, as it was for rationalism, the measure of the world, man was nevertheless the measure of all architecture; never did Le Corbusier think of architecture in terms of anything beyond man, anything purely political, social, or even religious. Thus the monastery of La Tourette was for him, "like the Chapel of Ronchamp, a program on the human scale." "Architecture," he had written twenty years earlier, "needs a human idiom." And the last twenty years of his life were devoted to the quest for an architectural idiom more universally human than that of the standards of Machine Age civilization. Chandigarh is the grandiose outcome of that quest.

Chandigarh: The Assembly Hall seen from the Secretariat, 1961.

Chandigarh: The Entrance of the Assembly Hall, 1961.

12 avril
52 (2)

GEOMETRY AND LIFE

THE spirit of geometry seems to find frequent expression in Le Corbusier's thinking. Doubtless his fidelity to the machine analogy as a method of exposition, if not of exploration, was first and foremost the result of pedagogic and polemical considerations. At the same time, there were evidently very deep roots to his contempt for the "donkey path," to his determination to provide a Gordian answer to the "law of meandering," to the tenacity with which he set about "classifying" everything, making everything "get back into line"; to his philosophy of standards and the plan, to his unremitting search for a universal system of proportions, to that glorification of the right angle which led him, in his old age, to dedicate an entire poem to its praises.

Yet, and with no less constancy, Le Corbusier never missed an opportunity of taking his distance from what is usually known as architectural rationalism. From the very outset of his career, he consistently refused to "express construction" in the spirit of a certain type of functionalism very much in fashion at the time. In 1927, when a violent campaign was on the point of being unleashed against the "soulless and

◄ *Final Design of the Governor's Palace at Chandigarh, April 12, 1952. Colored pen drawing. (Unexecuted project)*

homeless materialism" of the two "living-machines" that he was building in Stuttgart, he concluded a paper devoted to an examination of the state of architecture at that time with the following words: "The living-machine is on the road taken by architecture. It provides an unavoidable solution to the new equilibrium of a society centered on the machine. But, if the truth be told, a social equilibrium can exist only at the instigation of a credo, only through the manifestation of lyricism. To deny the credo, to suppress the lyricism, is first of all humanly impossible; and even if it were not so, it would be tantamount to depriving work of its very meaning, which is to serve... Where is architecture today? It is beyond the machine."

One could multiply the quotations in this sense. It was evidently over and beyond the modernism of function that Le Corbusier intended to situate architecture, *his* architecture, and well outside the clichés and dogmas of the academic school as well. "I do not accept the canons": the phrase occurs again and again, almost as a leitmotif, in the commentary he produced, twenty-seven years later, "from the user's point of view," on the Modulor scale—that scale in which one might otherwise be tempted to see the instrument of a process of rationalization, of integral standardization of the visual domain. No less categorical than his manner of setting up the regulatory virtues of "standards" against the uncertainties and betrayals of "sentiment" was his firm rejection of all measurement and all form imposed by purely mechanical, rule-of-thumb means. For him, a closed system of measurements or forms—a canon, a dogma, whether "modern" or "traditionalist"—could never provide more than a partial answer, limited and thus ineffective. "Open" solutions were alone capable of translating the interdependence, the solidarity of all the problems posed by the organization of man-occupied space; they alone preserved that indispensable element of "lyricism" which enabled the credo to intervene in creative fashion. In opposition to the principle of authority, ever since his early years in La Chaux-de-Fonds, he never tired of invoking the unique truth of first-hand experience, of the movement of life. "Passing down the line, you end up by knitting something together. I say 'knitting' because that means that all things are one in another, one implying another."

During the last twenty-five years of his career, the need for openness, the search for integrated solutions, became more and more insistent, manifesting itself in a wide variety of forms, from the multidisciplinary program of ASCORAL to the definition of the living scale of the Modulor, in the revival and further development of the evolutional theme (projects for a Museum of Unlimited Growth, housing groups in stepped clusters), as in the grid of the "7 Vs," a continuous network of traffic ways and exchanges, or in the passionate interest with which he welcomed new methods of construction, as well as the renewal of techniques relating to communication *(Electronic Poem)* and even the handling of information.

Yet it is fair to say that *all* his work, from the early years of *L'Esprit Nouveau* down to those of Chandigarh and Venice, was characterized by the great underlying themes of the continuity of construction, architecture, and urbanism, on the one hand, and the "synthesis of the major arts" (architecture, painting, sculpture), on the other—by the striving to integrate within one single movement the invention of architectural forms, the definition of urban structures, and the creation of "plastic objects" all equally in tune with the "lyricism of the new age."

While no doubt exists concerning either this empiricism or the sense that Le Corbusier had of belonging to this new age—a credo, a profession of faith in life which he took good care not to rationalize into an ideology of progress—the same cannot be said of the method or, as he preferred to call it, the way of thinking which guided his steps. On the one hand, unreserved acceptance of the discipline implicit in the "standard" as the dispenser of assurance; on the other, the unyielding demand for the liberty of "lyricism," conceived as the creative investigating force. This fundamental contradiction in Le Corbusier's thought cannot simply be resolved into the literary antinomies of classical "restraint" and Baroque "dynamism," still less into the conflict of Apollonian and Dionysian forces. Nor is it possible to single out in his work certain creations or periods governed by strict discipline, as against others representing so many liberations, or outbursts of lyricism. Measure, understood not as moderation or fear of excess but as a constant search for the unity of scale, and lyricism, understood not as the uncontrolled torrent of subjectivism but rather the peremptory eruption of intuitive vision—these two factors were indissolubly linked in his creative endeavor, and

"The 'words' of painting are by their very nature massive and full of meaning, expressing a notion rather than a quality. Their equivalents in the spoken language are words like sky, sea, rock, street, table, bread, door, house: they fix the species, as it were. They are fixed points which can enter unambiguously into an equation and there assume all possible qualities. For of such notion-words two or ten may be put together. From their presence, from their diverse contiguities, springs a relationship. It is precisely this relationship — a divergence, narrow or immense, between two exact notions side by side (or face to face) — that the artist discovers, the poet proclaims, the inspired create. It is like a light, a flash: it is a revelation, a shock. Such is the very raison d'être of the man who has the power to create" (Le Corbusier).

Bull VIII, 1954. Oil on canvas.

only the tension born of their conflicting demands maintained that paradoxical equilibrium from which each of his creations drew its dramatic intensity.

The fact is that, for Le Corbusier, "measure" and "lyricism" were not contradictory but complementary concepts; they represented two paths or two moments of a single approach to what he called biology, by which he understood the free, unopposed play of the laws of life. In the last resort, it is the ambiguity surrounding this latter notion that has been the source of the doubts and misunderstandings that have dogged that literary enterprise through which he sought to render a logical account of his visionary intuitions and creative achievements. Any thoroughgoing interpretation of Le Corbusier's thought would require the elucidation and clarification, one by one, of the many senses in which he used this word. "Life," at once a constrictive mechanism and a spontaneous source of invention, links man with Nature even when it allows, and even apparently demands, that he take his distance from it, as is the case in the urbanized world of the machine society. At all events, it was in "life" that Le Corbusier saw the supreme arbiter of every act of organization of the space occupied by man, the only one he recognized as having the right to judge his work. Here, too, his attitude was ambiguous. For instance, when asked what he, personally, thought of the changes made in the Pessac houses by their successive occupants—changes which strike the visitor, according to his tastes, as so many profanations or accusations (they certainly demonstrate the extraordinary flexibility of those very first "living-machines")—Le Corbusier was content to reply, in a phrase which often crossed his lips: "Life is always right!"

Resignation, veiled admission of defeat? Or the very opposite: the confident assurance that life would always end up by justifying him? Simply, no doubt, an unruffled readiness to await the verdict of an incorruptible judge.

It cannot be the task of this book to anticipate that judgment.

The following table makes no claim to completeness: it is a summary of dates and facts that will help the reader to a better understanding of Le Corbusier's work. Births are indicated by an asterisk, deaths by a cross. Le Corbusier's unexecuted projects are printed in small capitals.

DATES	GENERAL CHRONOLOGY	LE CORBUSIER: BIOGRAPHY AND PROJECTS
1880	Gustave Eiffel: Garabit Viaduct (1880-1884) * Guillaume Apollinaire, Franz Marc, Bruno Taut	
1881	* Picasso, Léger, Gleizes, Larionov	
1882	* Braque, Boccioni, Hugo Häring	
1883	* Walter Gropius, Theo van Doesburg	
1884	* Antoine Pevsner	
1885	Antoni Gaudí: Güell Palace, Barcelona (1885-1889) H.H. Richardson: Marshall Field Warehouse, Chicago (1885-1887) * Robert Delaunay, Henri Laurens, Vladimir Tatlin	
1886	* Amédée Ozenfant, Robert Mallet-Stevens, Ludwig Mies van der Rohe, Ernst May † H.H. Richardson	
1887	Gustave Eiffel: Eiffel Tower, Paris (1887-1889) * Blaise Cendrars, Juan Gris, Marcel Duchamp, Hans Arp, Kurt Schwitters, August Macke, Marc Chagall, Erich Mendelsohn	Birth on October 6, at La Chaux-de-Fonds (canton of Neuchâtel), Switzerland, of Charles-Edouard Jeanneret-Gris. He came of a family of watch-case enamellers and musicians, hailing originally from the Albi region of southern France
1888	Frank Lloyd Wright enters Louis Sullivan's office in Chicago (1888-1893) * Gerrit Thomas Rietveld, Antonio Sant'Elia, Hans Richter, Tristan Tzara, Giorgio de Chirico	
1889	Paris World's Fair (Eiffel Tower, Galerie des Machines) Burnham and Root: Monadnock Building, Chicago Camillo Sitte: *Der Städtebau nach seinen künstlerischen Grundsätzen*, Vienna * Hannes Meyer	
1890	* J.J.P. Oud, Naum Gabo, El Lissitzky	
1891	* Pier Luigi Nervi, Gio Ponti, Max Ernst	
1892	* André Lurçat, Richard Neutra	
1893	* Hans Scharoun	
1894	Anatole de Baudot: Saint-Jean de Montmartre, Paris Louis Sullivan: Guaranty Building, Buffalo	
1895	* Laszlo Moholy-Nagy, Richard Buckminster Fuller	
1896	Victor Horta: Maison du Peuple, Brussels (1896-1899) * Pierre Jeanneret, Frederick Kiesler	
1897	H.P. Berlage: Amsterdam Stock Exchange (1897-1903)	

DATES	GENERAL CHRONOLOGY	LE CORBUSIER: BIOGRAPHY AND PROJECTS
1898	Hector Guimard: Castel Béranger, Paris (1898-1899) Auguste Choisy: *Histoire de l'Architecture*, 2 vols., Paris Ebenezer Howard: *To-morrow: A Peaceful Path to Real Reform*, London (later retitled *Garden Cities of Tomorrow*) * J.H. van den Broek	
1899	Sullivan and Adler: Carson, Pirie & Scott Store, Chicago Astruc: Notre-Dame-du-Travail, Paris (1899-1901) * Maxwell Fry, Edoardo Torroja	
1900	Paris World's Fair Hector Guimard: Metro station entrances, Paris François Hennebique: apartment house, 1, rue Danton, Paris Antoni Gaudí: Güell Park, Barcelona (1900-1914)	Studies engraving at the Art School of La Chaux-de-Fonds. Influenced by his teacher, the painter L'Eplattenier, who was receptive to the contemporary Art Nouveau movement, and who encouraged his pupil to concentrate on architecture
1901	Henry van de Velde appointed head of the art schools in Weimar F.L. Wright: Prairie House project Julien Guadet: *Eléments et Théorie de l'Architecture*, Paris, 4 vols. (1901-1904) * Jean Prouvé, Konrad Wachsmann, Louis Kahn	
1902	A. Perret: apartment house, 25 bis, rue Franklin, Paris Henry van de Velde: Folkwang Museum, Hagen Camillo Sitte: *L'Art de bâtir les villes*, Paris (French translation of *Der Städtebau...*) * José Luis Sert, Lúcio Costa, Alf. Roth, Arne Jacobsen	Awarded a medal at the Turin Exhibition of Decorative Arts for a watch-case engraved in the Art Nouveau style
1903	Unwin and Parker: Letchworth, the first garden-city	
1904	Otto Wagner: Sparkasse, Vienna F.L. Wright: Larkin Building, Buffalo Tony Garnier: designs for an Industrial City (1901-1904) H. Muthesius: *Das engl. Haus*, 3 vols., Berlin (1904-1905) * Giuseppe Terragni	
1905	Frantz Jourdain: Samaritaine department store, Paris Josef Hoffmann: Stoclet House, Brussels (1905-1911) Robert Maillart: Upper Rhine bridge at Tavanasa (Grisons), Switzerland * Kunio Maekawa	Designs and builds his first house (Fallet House) at La Chaux-de-Fonds, followed by several others between now and 1916 (Schwob House). None of these were included in the publication of his "Complete Works." The Art School of La Chaux-de-Fonds now offers an advanced course on decorative art by L'Eplattenier
1906	Auguste Perret: Ponthieu Garage, Paris François Le Cœur: artists' studios, rue Cassini, Paris	
1907	Gropius enters the Berlin office of Peter Behrens, who has just been appointed architect and consultant to AEG (General Electricity Company) Founding of the *Deutscher Werkbund* Adolf Loos: Kärtner Bar, Vienna Eugène Freyssinet: Veurdre and Boutiron bridges Picasso: *Les Demoiselles d'Avignon* * Oscar Niemeyer	First travels: North Italy, Tuscany (discovery of the Carthusian monastery of Ema), Ravenna, Budapest and Vienna where he works for six months under Josef Hoffmann, leader of the Vienna Secession, who in 1903 had founded the Wiener Werkstätten (Vienna Workshops). Becomes acquainted with the ideas of Adolf Loos

DATES	GENERAL CHRONOLOGY	LE CORBUSIER: BIOGRAPHY AND PROJECTS
1908	Mies van der Rohe enters Behrens' office P. Behrens: AEG turbine factory (Turbinenhalle), Berlin Adolf Loos: *Ornament und Verbrechen*, Vienna H.P. Berlage: *Grundlagen u. Entwicklung der Architektur*, lectures given in Zurich, publ. in Rotterdam and Berlin * Max Bill	First stay in Paris, where he calls on Eugène Grasset, who advises him to go and see Auguste Perret In Lyons, where he meets Tony Garnier
1909	T. Garnier: La Mouche slaughterhouses, Lyons (1909/13) Garden-city of Hellerau, near Dresden F.L. Wright: Robie House, Chicago Marinetti: first Futurist manifesto	Second stay in Paris, where he works for fifteen months in Perret's office (February 1908-late 1909)
1910	Gropius leaves Behrens' office F.L. Wright exhibition in Berlin Exhibition of Islamic art in Munich Founding of *Der Sturm*, Berlin Perret: Théâtre des Champs-Elysées, Paris (1910-1913) Loos: Steiner House, Vienna Analytical Cubism * Eero Saarinen, Felix Candela	April 1910 to May 1911: Fellowship from the Art School of La Chaux-de-Fonds for the purpose of studying the arts and crafts movement in Germany. In Berlin he works for five months in the office of Peter Behrens, where he meets Gropius and Mies van der Rohe. Contacts with members of the Deutscher Werkbund and the Deutsche Werkstätten (in Munich, Theodor Fischer; in Berlin, Hermann Muthesius and Peter Behrens; in Dresden, Wolf Dohrn and Heinrich Tessenow; in Hagen, Karl Ernst Osthaus). Visit to Hellerau, near Dresden, where his brother Albert Jeanneret, a musician, is collaborating with Jaques-Dalcroze, who has opened a school of rhythmics here.
1911	Mies van der Rohe leaves Behrens' office and settles for a year in Holland (projected house for Mme Kröller, Otterlo) Gropius: Fagus Factory, Alfeld-an-der-Leine Georges Benoît-Lévy: *La cité-jardin*, 3 vols., Paris	Travels for seven months in Central Europe and the Balkans with his friend August Klipstein, an antique dealer in Bern: Vienna, the Danube, Budapest, Rumania, Turkey (Istanbul, Brussa), Greece (Mount Athos, Athens), Naples, Pompeii, Rome and Florence. An account of this journey, written at the time for the local newspaper in Chaux-de-Fonds, was published in book form in 1966 *(Voyage d'Orient)* The Art School of La Chaux-de-Fonds opens its "New Section," headed by L'Eplattenier
1912	Exhibitions: *Section d'Or* and *Italian Futurists*, Paris; *Blauer Reiter*, Munich; *Sonderbund*, Cologne François Le Cœur: Bergère Telephone Exchange, Paris H. Sauvage: tiered apartment house, rue Vavin, Paris Max Berg: Jahrhunderthalle, Breslau (1912-1913) Gleizes and Metzinger: *Du cubisme*, Paris	In charge of courses on arch. and furniture in the "New Section" of the Art School of La Ch.-de-Fds. (1912-1913) His observations on the German movement published in an official report *(Etude sur le mouvement d'art décoratif en Allemagne*, La Chaux-de-Fonds*)* Trips to Paris, where he exhibits in the Salon d'Automne a set of watercolors (1907-1913) illustrating his travels, under the title: *Langage de pierres*
1913	Founding of the *Schweizerischer Werkbund* F.L. Wright: Midway Gardens, Chicago Patrick Geddes: *Cities in Evolution*, London French translation of *Ornament and Crime* by A. Loos * Kenzo Tange	
1914	*Deutscher Werkbund* Exhibition, Cologne (Bruno Taut: glass pavilion - Gropius and Adolf Meyer: model factory - Van de Velde: theater)	Head of the "Ateliers d'Art Réunis," which executes several sets of interior decorations in the La Chaux-de-Fonds region

DATES	GENERAL CHRONOLOGY	LE CORBUSIER: BIOGRAPHY AND PROJECTS
1914	A. Sant'Elia: *Manifesto dell'Architettura Futurista*, Florence * Jakob B. Bakema	DOM-INO HOUSES
1915	Malevich: *Black Square* (possibly 1913)	
1916	Eugène Freyssinet: Airship hangars, Orly (1916-1924) F.L. Wright: Imperial Hotel, Tokyo (1916-1922) Anatole de Baudot: *L'Architecture et le béton armé*, Paris	Builds his last house at La Chaux-de-Fonds (Schwob House) SEASIDE VILLA FOR PAUL POIRET
1917	Launching of the Dutch magazine *De Stijl*, Leyden (1917-1931) Dada movement begins in Zurich J.J.P. Oud: seafront at Scheveningen	Settles in Paris, at 20, rue Jacob, where he lives for the next seventeen years. At Perret's office he meets the painter Amédée Ozenfant
1918	*Arbeitsrat für Kunst*, Berlin * Paul Rudolph † Otto Wagner	Paints his first pictures First exhibition, with Ozenfant, where they launch the manifesto of Purism: *Après le Cubisme*
1919	Launching of the magazine *Wendingen*, Amsterdam (1919-1925) Gropius founds the Bauhaus, Weimar *Novembergruppe*, Berlin M. v. der Rohe: projects for glass skyscrapers (1919-1922) Tatlin: projected monument to the Third International (1919-1920)	INDUSTRIALIZED HOUSING FOR TROYES
1920	Van Doesburg visits Paris Erich Mendelsohn: Einstein Tower, Potsdam Piet Mondrian: *Le Néo-Plasticisme*, Paris Naum Gabo and Antoine Pevsner: *Constructivist Manifesto*, Moscow	With Ozenfant and Paul Dermée, he begins publishing a magazine, *L'Esprit Nouveau, revue d'esthétique* (renamed, after several numbers, *L'Esprit Nouveau, revue de l'activité contemporaine*): 28 issues appear between 1920 and 1925 Signs a series of articles (later published in book form as *Vers une architecture*) under the name of one of his ancestors, Le Corbusier-Saugnier CITROHAN HOUSE NO. 1 - MONOL HOUSES
1921	Van Doesburg lectures at Weimar, where he makes his home until 1923 Theo van Doesburg: *Classique - Baroque - Moderne*, Paris (French translation of *Klassiek, barok, modern*, The Hague 1920) Adolf Loos: *Ins Leere gesprochen 1897-1900*, Paris † François Hennebique	Exhibits at the Galerie Druet. Le Corbusier and Ozenfant advise Raoul La Roche at the time of the Kahnweiler sales, helping him to build up his collection of Cubist pictures
1922	Auguste Perret: Church at Le Raincy (1922-1923) El Lissitzky starts the magazine *Veshch* (Object,) Berlin Malevich begins writing *Suprematism* (1922-1924), published in German (1927) in the series of Bauhaus Books under the title "Die gegenstandslose Welt" Exhibition of contemporary Russian art, Berlin	Opens an architect's office with his cousin Pierre Jeanneret, who remains in partnership with him till 1940. Installs his office in the corridor of a former Jesuit monastery at 35, rue de Sèvres—his headquarters for the rest of his life Exhibits at the Salon d'Automne (Citrohan house and Contemporary City) and the Salon des Indépendants CITROHAN HOUSE NO. 2, MULTISTORY VILLAS (IMMEUBLE-VILLAS), CONTEMPORARY CITY FOR THREE MILLION INHABITANTS

DATES	GENERAL CHRONOLOGY	LE CORBUSIER: BIOGRAPHY AND PROJECTS
1923	Exhibition of Neo-Plasticist architectural projects, Galerie Léonce Rosenberg, Paris (later shown at Nancy and in 1924 at Weimar) Adolf Loos settles in Paris (1923-1928) Bauhaus Week, Weimar Laszlo Moholy-Nagy joins the Bauhaus Albert Gleizes: *La peinture et ses lois ; ce qui devait sortir du cubisme* Gropius: *Idee und Aufbau des staatlichen Bauhauses* Erich Mendelsohn: *Dynamik und Funktion*, lecture given at Amsterdam Mies van der Rohe, H. Richter and W. Graeff start the magazine *G - Material zur elementaren Gestaltung*, Berlin † Gustave Eiffel	Exhibition of his paintings at the Galerie Léonce Rosenberg Publication of *Vers une architecture*
1924	Competition for the design of the *Chicago Tribune Tower* G.T. Rietveld: Schröder House, Utrecht J.J.P. Oud: low-cost housing, Hook of Holland First tubular steel furniture (Marcel Breuer, Mart Stam, Mies van der Rohe) † Louis Sullivan	First volume of his *Œuvre Complète* published by Jean Badovici (Ed. A. Morancé, Paris). Publication is broken off in 1938 after the eighth volume (*Œuvre plastique*) STANDARDIZED HOUSE ARTISANS' HOUSES
1925	International Exhibition of Decorative Art, Paris Owing to right-wing political hostility, the Bauhaus is transferred from Weimar to Dessau, occupying new buildings designed by Gropius (1925-1926) J.J.P. Oud: Kiefhoek housing scheme, Rotterdam (1925-1930) First volumes of the series of Bauhaus Books El Lissitzky and Hans Arp: *Die Kunstismen*, Berlin	*L'Esprit Nouveau* ceases publication. Parts company with Ozenfant Pierre A. Emery works in his office Publishes *La peinture moderne* (with Ozenfant), *L'Art décoratif d'aujourd'hui* and *Urbanisme* VOISIN PLAN FOR PARIS VILLA FOR MME MEYER UNIVERSITY CITY
1926	Adolf Loos: Tristan Tzara House, Paris Robert Mallet-Stevens: rue Mallet-Stevens, Paris André Lurçat: Guggenbühl House, Paris (1926-1927) Theo van Doesburg, Sophie Täuber and Hans Arp: decorations, *Aubette* dance hall, Strasbourg (1926-1928) Eileen Gray and Jean Badovici: villa at Cap-Martin Piet Mondrian: *The Home, the Street, the City*, Paris Adolf Behne: *Der moderne Zweckbau*, Munich *Der Ring*, association of progressive architects, Berlin Martin Wagner becomes City Architect of Berlin Ernst May: Römerstadt suburb, Frankfort (1926-1928) † Antoni Gaudí	Death of Le Corbusier's father Publishes *Almanach d'architecture moderne* MINIMUM HOUSES
1927	Weissenhof housing exhibition, Stuttgart Hannes Meyer: German Trade Unions School, Bernau/Berlin (1928-1930) Erich Mendelsohn: department stores at Breslau, Chemnitz, Stuttgart - Matté Trucco: Fiat Plant, Turin Richard Buckminster Fuller: first Dymaxion House	Competition for the League of Nations building in Geneva: Le Corbusier's project is awarded a prize but rejected as a result of intrigue LEAGUE OF NATIONS BUILDING, GENEVA
1928	First International Congress of Modern Architecture (CIAM), Château de La Sarraz, near Lausanne Gropius resigns as director of the Bauhaus, being succeeded by Hannes Meyer	Lecture tour in South America Journey to Moscow In his painting, beginning of the period of "objects of poetic reaction"

DATES	GENERAL CHRONOLOGY	LE CORBUSIER: BIOGRAPHY AND PROJECTS
1928	First Italian Exhibition of *Rational Architecture*, Rome Brinkmann, van der Vlugt and Mart Stam: Van Nelle tobacco factory, Rotterdam (1928-1930) Rudolf Steiner: *Goetheanum*, Dornach, near Basel Clarence Stein: garden city of Radburn, New Jersey Amédée Ozenfant: *Art*, Paris Sigfried Giedion: *Bauen in Frankreich, Eisen, Eisenbeton*, Leipzig	Alfred Roth works in his office Lecture on Le Corbusier given in Berlin by Fernand Léger Violent anti-Le Corbusier pamphlet by the Genevese architect Alexandre de Senger: *Le Cheval de Troie du bolchévisme*, Bienne WANNER BUILDINGS, GENEVA
1929	Second CIAM congress, Frankfort *(Die Wohnung für das Existenzminimum*, Stuttgart 1930) Mies van der Rohe: German Pavilion for the International Exhibition in Barcelona Alvar Aalto: Paimio Sanatorium, Finland (1929-1934) Richard Neutra: Lovell House, Los Angeles Theo van Doesburg: house at Meudon (1929-1931) Bruno Taut: *Die neue Baukunst in Europa und Amerika*, Stuttgart (written in 1924)	First trip to Algiers Kunio Maekawa and J.L. Sert work in his office First volume of the Zurich edition of *Le Corbusier: Œuvre Complète*, published by Walter Boesiger (Editions Girsberger, Zurich). Completed in seven volumes in 1965 HOUSE FOR MR. X, BRUSSELS LOUCHEUR HOUSES "MUNDANEUM" AND WORLD CITY, GENEVA
1930	Third CIAM congress, Brussels *(Rationelle Bebauungsweisen*, Stuttgart 1931) Mies succeeds Hannes Meyer as director of the Bauhaus German section, organized for the *Werkbund* by Gropius and Moholy-Nagy, at the Salon des Artistes Décorateurs, Paris Hannes Meyer and Ernst May settle in the U.S.S.R. Mies van der Rohe: Tugendhat House, Brno G. Pingusson: Hotel Latitude 43, Saint-Tropez (1930-1933) G.A. Platz: *Die Baukunst der neuesten Zeit*, Berlin Alberto Sartoris: *Gli Elementi dell' Architettura razionale*, Milan	Le Corbusier becomes a French citizen. He marries Yvonne Gallis The human figure makes its appearance in his painting Takes part in *Cercle et Carré* Charlotte Perriand and Brechbühler work in his office Publishes *Précisions sur un état présent de l'architecture et de l'urbanisme* TOWN-PLANNING SCHEME FOR ALGIERS (PLAN A)
1931	Second Italian Exhibition of Rational Architecture, Rome Pierre Chareau and B. Bijvoet: Dalsace House, Paris André Lurçat: Karl Marx School, Villejuif, near Paris Rockefeller Center, New York The Paris magazine *L'Architecture d'aujourd'hui* begins publication † Theo van Doesburg	Contributes to the magazine *Plans* (1931-1932) J. Bossu, G. Kepes, Sakakura and O. Senn work in his office Senger's pamphlet, translated into German *(Die Brandfackel Moskaus)*, becomes one of the basic texts in the Nazi campaign against modern architecture MUSEUM OF CONTEMPORARY ART, PARIS PALACE OF THE SOVIETS, MOSCOW ERRAZURIS HOUSE, CHILE
1932	Bauhaus transferred from Dessau to Berlin Bruno Taut moves to Moscow Giuseppe Terragni: Casa del Fascio, Como Bentwood chairs designed by Alvar Aalto International Exhibition of Modern Architecture, Museum of Modern Art, New York H.R. Hitchcock and Philip Johnson: *The International Style: Architecture since 1922*, New York First manifestos of the *Structural Study Associates*, written by Buckminster Fuller	Louis Hourticq, a member of the Institut, and Umbdenstock, a professor at the Ecole des Beaux-Arts and the Ecole Polytechnique, organize a public meeting at the Salle Wagram in Paris to protest against the baneful influence of Le Corbusier RENTENANSTALT, ZURICH

DATES	GENERAL CHRONOLOGY	LE CORBUSIER: BIOGRAPHY AND PROJECTS
1933	Bauhaus closed down by the Nazis Erich Mendelsohn leaves Germany Bruno Taut leaves the U.S.S.R. for Japan Beaudouin and Lods: two development estates near Paris (Cité de La Muette, Drancy, and Cité du Chant des Oiseaux, Bagneux) Emil Kaufmann: *Von Ledoux bis Le Corbusier,* Vienna † Adolf Loos	Contributes to the magazine *Préludes* Publishes *Croisade, ou le crépuscule des académies* L. Miquel works in his office Violent attack on Le Corbusier in *L'Architecture va-t-elle mourir?* by Camille Mauclair MACIA HOUSING ESTATE, BARCELONA DURAND HOUSING ESTATE, ALGIERS APARTMENT HOUSE, ALGIERS PLAN FOR THE LEFT BANK OF THE SCHELDT, ANTWERP
1934	Fourth CIAM congress on board the *Patris* between Marseilles and Piraeus *(Athens Charter)* Gropius leaves Germany for England Hannes Meyer and Ernst May leave the U.S.S.R. F.L. Wright: first Usonian house (Willey House, Minneapolis) † H.P. Berlage	Takes a leading part in writing the *Athens Charter* of the CIAM PLANS FOR ALGIERS (PLANS B AND C) PLAN FOR NEMOURS, ALGERIA THE RADIANT FARM
1935	Alfred Roth and Marcel Breuer: Doldertal apartments, Zurich (1935-1936) † Kasimir Malevich	First visit to the United States at the invitation of the Museum of Modern Art in New York Mural paintings at Vézelay (Badovici House) Exhibition of so-called primitive art organized by Louis Carré in Le Corbusier's studio at 24, rue Nungesser-et-Coli, Paris Publishes *La Ville Radieuse* and *Air Craft* (London) TWO MUSEUMS OF MODERN ART, PARIS PLANS FOR HELLOCOURT, FRANCE, AND THE VALLEY OF ZLIN, CZECHOSLOVAKIA
1936	Alvar Aalto: paper mill, Sunila, Finland (1936-1939) F.L. Wright: Kaufmann House, *Falling Water,* Bear Run, Pa., and Johnson Wax Company administration building, Racine, Wis. Nikolaus Pevsner: *Pioneers of the Modern Movement from William Morris to Walter Gropius,* London	Second journey to South America ILOT INSALUBRE NO. 6, PARIS PLAN FOR PARIS (FOR THE 1937 WORLD'S FAIR) APARTMENT BLOCK, BASTION KELLERMANN, PARIS UNIVERSITY CITY, RIO DE JANEIRO
1937	Fifth CIAM congress, Paris *(Logis et Loisirs,* Paris 1938*)* Paris World's Fair Mies van der Rohe leaves Germany and settles in Chicago Gropius moves to the United States, becoming Professor of Architecture at Harvard Beaudouin, Lods and Prouvé: Maison du Peuple, Clichy, Paris	Publishes *Quand les cathédrales étaient blanches : Voyage au pays des timides* RECREATION CENTER FOR 100,000 PEOPLE, PARIS VAILLANT-COUTURIER MONUMENT, VILLEJUIF, NEAR PARIS PROJECT FOR A WATER EXHIBITION AT LIÈGE, BELGIUM, IN 1939
1938	Pier Luigi Nervi: military hangars at Orbetello Lewis Mumford: *The Culture of Cities,* New York † Bruno Taut	Mural paintings at Cap-Martin (Badovici House) Exhibition of Le Corbusier's sculpture at the Kunsthaus, Zurich Publishes *Des canons, des munitions? Merci... des logis s.v.p.!* (Guns, munitions? No thanks, houses please) PALACE OF JUSTICE, ALGIERS LA MARINE SKYSCRAPER, ALGIERS CARTESIAN SKYSCRAPER COOPERATIVE VILLAGE MASTER PLAN FOR BUENOS AIRES FRENCH PAVILION FOR A WORLD'S FAIR

DATES	GENERAL CHRONOLOGY	LE CORBUSIER: BIOGRAPHY AND PROJECTS
1939	New York World's Fair Robert Le Ricolais appointed professor at the University of Pennsylvania	Publishes *Le lyrisme des temps nouveaux et l'urbanisme* André Wogenscky begins working under Le Corbusier MUSEUM OF UNLIMITED GROWTH CLARKE-ARUNDELL HOUSE PLAN FOR THE VAR VALLEY, SOUTHERN FRANCE
1940	† Robert Maillart	HOUSES FOR LANNEMEZAN - M.A.S. HOUSES MURONDINS CONSTRUCTIONS - FLYING SCHOOLS
1941	Erich Mendelsohn settles in the United States S. Giedion: *Space, Time & Architecture*, Cambridge, Mass. † Robert Delaunay, El Lissitzky	Publishes *Destin de Paris* and *Sur les Quatre Routes*
1942	Mies van der Rohe: first buildings of the Illinois Institute of Technology, Chicago José Luis Sert: *Can Our Cities Survive?*, Cambridge, Mass.	Begins working out his Modulor system of design Publishes *Les constructions Murondins* *La Maison des Hommes* (with François de Pierrefeu) LA MARINE SKYSCRAPER, ALGIERS (PROJECT B) MASTER PLAN FOR ALGIERS
1943	† Giuseppe Terragni	Founds the Association of Designers for an Architectural Renewal (ASCORAL) Publishes *La Charte d'Athènes* (with a preface by Jean Giraudoux) and *Entretien avec les étudiants des écoles d'architecture* LINEAR INDUSTRIAL CITY - GREEN FACTORY
1944	† Piet Mondrian, Aristide Maillol	Aujame works in his office TRANSITORY APARTMENT BLOCK
1945		*Manière de penser l'Urbanisme* Soltan works in his office Traveling exhibition in the United States, organized by the Walker Art Center, Minneapolis PLAN FOR THE RECONSTRUCTION OF SAINT-DIÉ, FRANCE
1946	Gropius founds *The Architects Collaborative* (T.A.C.) Mies van der Rohe: Farnsworth House, Fox River, Ill. (1946-1951)	*Les Trois Etablissements Humains, Propos d'Urbanisme* V. Bodiansky and G. Candilis work in his office PLAN FOR THE RECONSTRUCTION OF LA PALLICE, NEAR LA ROCHELLE
1947	Sixth CIAM congress at Bridgwater, England	In New York as a member of the commission of architects chosen to design the United Nations headquarters Mural painting in his rue de Sèvres offices UNITED NATIONS HEADQUARTERS, NEW YORK
1948	F.L. Wright: first circular house (second house for Herbert Jacobs, Middleton, Wis.) Sigfried Giedion: *Mechanization Takes Command*, New York	Final working out of his Modulor system of design Mural in Swiss Pavilion, Cité Universitaire, Paris Wood carvings with Joseph Savina Publishes *New World of Space* (New York) Traveling exhibition in the United States, organized by the Institute of Contemporary Art, Boston PILGRIMAGE CENTER, SAINTE-BAUME, SOUTHERN FRANCE
1949	Walter Gropius (T.A.C.): Harvard Graduate Center	S. Woods and I. Xenakis work in his office ROB AND ROQ VACATION HOUSES, CAP-MARTIN

DATES	GENERAL CHRONOLOGY	LE CORBUSIER: BIOGRAPHY AND PROJECTS
1950	Arne Jacobsen: houses at Klampenborg, Denmark Miquel and Bourlier: Aérohabitat, Algiers	*Le Modulor* and *Poésie sur Alger* PILOT PLAN FOR BOGOTA
1951	Eighth CIAM congress at Hoddesdon, England Candilis, Woods and ATBAT-Afrique: Arab housing, Casablanca	Appointed architectural counsellor to the government of the Punjab for the construction of the new capital at Chandigarh Studies for the Chastang dam Tapestry designs with Pierre Baudouin Sand sculptures at the home of Tino Nivola on Long Island A. Maisonnier works in his office ROTTERDAM DISTRICT, STRASBOURG
1952	Breuer, Nervi, Zehrfuss: UNESCO Building, Paris (1952-1957) Mies van der Rohe: Crown Hall, Illinois Institute of Technology, Chicago Skidmore, Owings and Merrill: Lever House, New York	Begins painting the series of *Bulls* THE PEON'S HOUSE, CHANDIGARH, INDIA PLAN FOR MARSEILLE-SUD
1953	Ninth CIAM congress at Aix-en-Provence † Erich Mendelsohn	Exhibition of his sculpture, Musée d'Art Moderne, Paris Violent attack on his Marseilles apartment block by Lewis Mumford in *The New Yorker*
1954	Alison and Peter Smithson: Hunstanton School, Norfolk, England † Auguste Perret, Henri Laurens, Henri Matisse	*Une petite maison* published in Zurich Exhibition at the Kunsthalle, Bern THE OPEN HAND, CHANDIGARH
1955	M. Bill: buildings of the Hochschule für Gestaltung, Ulm Eero Saarinen: General Motors Technical Center, Warren, Mich., and Kresge Auditorium, Massachusetts Institute of Technology, Cambridge Frei Otto: suspended roofs for the Federal Flower Show, Cassel † Fernand Léger	Paints his first *Icon* *Le Poème de l'Angle Droit*, with 19 color lithographs (Paris) *Modulor 2* NEW RESIDENTIAL DISTRICT, MEAUX
1956	Tenth CIAM congress at Dubrovnik, Yugoslavia Lúcio Costa: master plan for Brasilia London County Council: Roehampton housing estate F.L. Wright: Guggenheim Museum, New York (1956-1959) Eero Saarinen: T.W.A. Terminal, Kennedy Airport, New York (1956-1962) H. Scharoun: Berlin Philharm. Concert Hall (1956-1963) Jörn Utzon: first project for the Sydney Opera House † Vladimir Tatlin	*Les plans Le Corbusier pour Paris 1956-1962* GOVERNOR'S PALACE, CHANDIGARH
1957	Interbau Exhibition, Berlin (Hansa district) Marcello d'Olivio: children's village, Trieste (Villa Opicina) † Henry van de Velde	First exhibition at La Chaux-de-Fonds (tapestries, *Poem of the Right Angle*) Death of his wife Yvonne Retrospective exhibition at the Kunsthaus, Zurich
1958	Brussels World's Fair Louis Kahn: Richards Medical Research Building, University of Pennsylvania, Philadelphia (1958-1960) Mies van der Rohe: Seagram Building, New York	*Electronic Poem* with music by Edgar Varèse for the Philips Pavilion at the Brussels World's Fair METAL RURAL HOUSING, LAGNY (WITH JEAN PROUVÉ) RECONSTRUCTION OF THE CENTER OF BERLIN

DATES	GENERAL CHRONOLOGY	LE CORBUSIER: BIOGRAPHY AND PROJECTS
1958	Eero Saarinen: Yale Hockey Rink, New Haven, Conn. Pier Luigi Nervi and Gio Ponti: Pirelli Tower, Milan Belgioioso, Peressutti, Rogers: Velasca Tower, Milan Buckminster Fuller: Geodesic Dome, Union Tank Car Co., Baton Rouge, La. Paul Rudolph becomes Chairman of the Department of Architecture at Yale University	
1959	Collapse and break-up of CIAM at the eleventh congress in Otterlo, Holland Oscar Niemeyer: government buildings in Brasilia Atelier 5: Halen estate, near Bern Vittoriano Viganò: Istituto Marchiondi, Milan Arne Jacobsen: S.A.S. Building, Copenhagen Pier Luigi Nervi: halls for the Olympic Games, Rome † Frank Lloyd Wright	
1960		*L'Atelier de la Recherche Patiente* *Petites Confidences* (10 lithographs) Death of Le Corbusier's mother at the age of 100 ELECTRONIC DECISIONS CENTER, CHANDIGARH
1961	Park Hill housing estate, Sheffield Kallmann, McKinnel and Knowles: town hall project, Boston Jane Jacobs: *The Death and Life of Great American Cities*, New York † Blaise Cendrars, Edoardo Torroja	Tapestry designs for the Law Courts (Palace of Justice) at Chandigarh
1962	Frei Otto: *Zugbeanspruchte Konstruktionen*, Berlin † Eugène Freyssinet	Retrospective exhibition, Musée d'Art Moderne, Paris Large enamelled iron door for the Assembly Hall at Chandigarh EXHIBITION HALL, STOCKHOLM
1963	Kenzo Tange: halls for the Olympic Games, Tokyo Candilis, Woods and Josic: project for Free University, Berlin R. Simounet: University City, Tananarive, Madagascar † J.J.P. Oud, Georges Braque	Retrospective exhibition at the Palazzo Strozzi, Florence HOTEL ON THE SITE OF THE GARE D'ORSAY, PARIS OLIVETTI ELECTRONIC COMPUTER CENTER, RHO, MILAN INTERNATIONAL ART CENTER, ERLENBACH, FRANKFORT CHURCH AT FIRMINY, NEAR LYONS
1964	Swiss National Exhibition, Lausanne	CONGRESS HALL, STRASBOURG
1965	† Frederick Kiesler	August 27, sudden death of Le Corbusier while bathing at Cap-Martin HOSPITAL, VENICE - FRENCH EMBASSY, BRASILIA MUSEUM OF THE 20TH CENTURY, NANTERRE, NEAR PARIS
1966	† Amédée Ozenfant	
1967	International Exhibition (Expo 1967), Montreal Moshe Shafdie: *Housing* † Pierre Jeanneret	Opening of the Le Corbusier Center, Zurich
1968		Creation of the Le Corbusier Foundation, Paris

1916 - Schwob House, La Chaux-de-Fonds

1922 - Ozenfant House, Paris

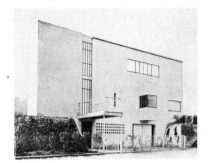

1922 - Villa, Vaucresson, near Paris

1923 - La Roche and Jeanneret Houses, Paris

1924 - Lipchitz and Miestschaninoff Houses, Boulogne sur Seine

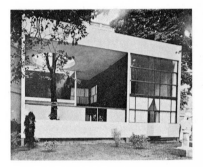

1925 - L'Esprit Nouveau Pavilion, International Exhibition of Decorative Art, Paris

1925 - Pessac housing development, Bordeaux

1925 - House for his parents, Corseaux-Vevey, Lake of Geneva

1926 - Ternisien House, Boulogne sur Seine

1926 - Cook House, Boulogne sur Seine

1926 - Guiette House, Antwerp

1926 - "Palais du Peuple" of the Salvation Army,
Paris

1927 - Villa Stein, Garches, near Paris

1927 - Two houses for the Weissenhof housing exhibition, Stuttgart

1927 - Plainex House, Paris

1928 - Nestlé exhibition stand, Paris

1929 - Villa at Carthage, Tunisia

1929 - Remodelling and enlarging of the Church House, Ville-d'Avray, near Paris

1929 - Easychair, example of the furniture (chairs and cabinets) exhibited with Pierre Jeanneret and Charlotte Perriand at the Salon d'Automne, Paris

1931 - Villa Savoye, Poissy, near Paris

1931 - Villa for Mme de Mandrot, Le Pradet, near Toulon

1931 - Penthouse apartment for Charles de Beistegui, Champs-Elysées, Paris

1931 - Salvation Army Hostel (remodelled river boat), Paris

1932 - Apartment building (Immeuble Clarté or Maison de Verre), Geneva

1932 - Swiss Pavilion, Cité Universitaire, Paris

1933 - Salvation Army Hostel (Cité de Refuge), Paris

1933 - Apartment house, 24, rue Nungesser-et-Coli, Paris

1933 - Le Corbusier's own apartment and studio, 24, rue Nungesser-et-Coli, Paris

1933 - Ministry of Light Industry (now Centro-soyuz), Moscow

1935 - Summer house, Les Mathes

1935 - Weekend house, La Celle-Saint-Cloud, near Paris

1937 - Les Temps Nouveaux Pavilion, Paris World's Fair

1938 - Plans of the Ministry of Education, Rio de Janeiro, with Lucio Costa and Oscar Niemeyer (finished in 1943)

1940 - La France d'Outremer exhibition, Paris

1949 - House of Dr Currutchet, Buenos Aires

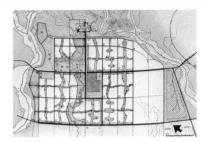

1951 - Town-plan for Chandigarh, India

1952 - Apartment block (Unité d'Habitation),
Marseilles

1952 - Duval Plant, Saint-Dié

1952 - Cabin at Cap-Martin, French Riviera

1953 - Church of Ronchamp, near Belfort

1953 - Apartment block (Unité d'Habitation),
Nantes-Rezé

1954 - Building of the Mill-Owners' Association,
Ahmedabad, India

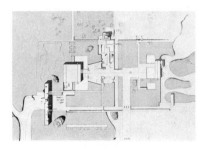

1955 - Plan of the Capitol, Chandigarh

1955 - Sarabhai House, Ahmedabad

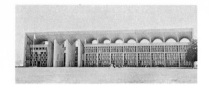

1956 - Palace of Justice, Chandigarh

1956 - Shodan House, Ahmedabad

1957 - Ahmedabad Museum

1957 - Jaoul Houses, Neuilly-sur-Seine

1958 - Apartment block (Unité d'Habitation), Berlin

1958 - Philips Pavilion, Brussels World's Fair

1958 - Secretariat, Chandigarh

1959 - Dominican Monastery of Sainte-Marie de La Tourette, Eveux, near Lyons

1959 - Museum of Modern Western Art, Tokyo

1959 - Brazilian Pavilion, Cité Universitaire, Paris

1959 - Apartment block (Unité d'Habitation), Briey-en-Forêt

1961 - Assembly Hall, Chandigarh

1964 - Carpenter Center for the Visual Arts, Harvard University, Cambridge, Mass.

1965 - House of Culture, Firminy, near Lyons

1967 - Exhibition hall, Zurich

1968 - Apartment block (Unité d'Habitation), Firminy

213

POISSY

SAINT-GERMAIN   PARIS

Villa Savoye
Chemin de Villiers

Jaoul House
83, Rue de Longchamp, Neuilly-sur-Seine

Salvation Army Hostel
12, Rue Cantagrel

La Roche and Jeanneret Houses
8-10, Square du Docteur-Blanche

Villa Stein
17, Rue du Prof.-Victor-Pauchet, Garches

Cook House
6, Rue Denfert-Rochereau, Boulogne-sur-Seine

Ozenfant House
53, Avenue Reille

Plainex House
Boulevard Masséna

Apartment House
24, Rue Nungesser-et-Coli

Swiss Pavilion and Brazilian Pavilion
Cité Universitaire
7, Boulevard Jourdan

Salvation Army, Palais du Peuple
29, Rue des Cordelières

BIBLIOGRAPHY

All the books devoted to Le Corbusier include a more or less extensive bibliography up to the date of publication. The following may also be consulted: "Le Corbusier," article by Maurice BESSET in *Encyclopedia of World Art*, Vol. IX, McGraw-Hill, New York, Toronto, London 1964; *Le Corbusier, Bibliografia generale*, by Carmen GREGOTTI, in the catalogue of an exhibition of books and drawings by Le Corbusier, Feltrinelli, Milan-Rome, n.d.

These two bibliographies are limited to books and special numbers of magazines either published by Le Corbusier himself or devoted to him. This is not the case for:

Le Corbusier e l'Italia, bibliography by Italo INSOLERA, Alberto SAMONÀ and Luisa FANGLI, in *L'Opera di Le Corbusier*, catalogue of the exhibition at the Palazzo Strozzi, Florence 1963, which gives a complete bibliography to that date of the Italian translations of Le Corbusier's writings and of the books and principal magazine articles devoted to him in Italy. So far nothing comparable exists for any other country.

The "Fondation Le Corbusier" (10, square du Dr Blanche, Paris 16) is at present preparing a complete bibliography and would be grateful to anyone who can supply it with pertinent information.

Writings by Le Corbusier

Early writings:

Le Voyage d'Orient, Forces Vives, Paris 1966 (reissue of newspaper articles published in 1911 in *La Feuille d'Avis de La Chaux-de-Fonds*). — *Etude sur le mouvement d'art décoratif en Allemagne*, Haefeli & Cie, La Chaux-de-Fonds 1912 (rapport présenté à la Commission de l'Ecole d'art de La Chaux-de-Fonds par Monsieur Ch. E. Jeanneret, architecte, sur les observations qu'il a eu l'occasion de faire en Allemagne durant son séjour d'avril 1910 à mai 1911). — *Après le Cubisme* (with Amédée OZENFANT), Editions des Commentaires, Paris 1918.

"L'Esprit Nouveau" Series:

Vers une architecture, Crès, Paris 1923 (reissue, Vincent, Fréal & Cie, Paris 1958). In English: *Towards a New Architecture*, tr. by Frederick Etchells, John Rodko Publisher, London 1927. — *La Peinture moderne* (with OZENFANT), Crès, Paris 1925. — *Urbanisme*, Crès, Paris 1925 (reissue, Vincent, Fréal & Cie, Paris 1966, preface by Jean CASSOU). In English: *The City of To-morrow and its Planning*, tr. from the 8th ed. by Frederick Etchells, Architectural Press, London 1947. — *L'Art décoratif d'aujourd'hui*, Crès, Paris 1925 (reissue, Vincent, Fréal & Cie, Paris 1959). — *Almanach d'Architecture moderne*, Crès, Paris 1926. — *Une maison, un palais*, Crès, Paris 1928. — *Précisions sur un état présent de l'architecture et de l'urbanisme*, avec un prologue américain, un corollaire brésilien, suivi d'une température parisienne et d'une atmosphère moscovite, Crès, Paris 1930 (reissue, Vincent, Fréal & Cie, Paris 1960). — *Croisade, ou le crépuscule des académies*, Crès, Paris 1933.

Publications 1935-1945:

Air Craft, The Studio, London 1935. — *La Ville radieuse*, Editions de l'Architecture d'Aujourd'hui, Boulogne-sur-Seine 1935 (reissue, Vincent, Fréal & Cie, Paris 1964). In English: *The Radiant City*, tr. by Pamela Wright, Eleanor Levieux and Derek Coltmann, Orion Press, New York 1965. — *Quand les cathédrales étaient blanches: Voyage au pays des timides*, Plon, Paris 1937 (paperback, Gonthier, Paris 1965). In English: *When the Cathedrals Were White*, tr. by Francis E. Hyslop, Jr., Reynal and Hitchcock, New York 1947; paperback, McGraw-Hill, New York, Toronto, London 1964. — *Des canons, des munitions? Merci! Des logis... svp.*, Editions de l'Architecture d'Aujourd'hui, Boulogne-sur-Seine 1938. — *Le lyrisme des temps nouveaux et l'urbanisme*, Le Point, Colmar 1939. — *Sur les quatre routes*, N.R.F., Paris 1941. In English: *The Four Routes*, tr. by Dorothy Todd, Dennis Dobson Ltd, London

1947. — *La maison des hommes* (with François de Pierrefeu), Plon, Paris 1942. In English: *The Home of Man*, tr. by Clive Entwistle and Gordon Holt, Architectural Press, London 1948. — *Entretien avec les étudiants des écoles d'architecture*, Denoel, Paris 1943. In English: *Talks with Students from the Schools of Architecture*, tr. by Pierre Chase, Orion Press, New York 1961. — *Urbanisme des CIAM, La Charte d'Athènes* (with the CIAM Group, France), foreword by Jean Giraudoux, Plon, Paris 1943. — *Manière de penser l'urbanisme*, Editions de l'Architecture d'Aujourd'hui, Boulogne-sur-Seine n.d. (1945).

Publications 1945-1965:

Les Trois Etablissements humains, Denoel, Paris 1946. — *Propos d'Urbanisme*, Bourrelier & Cie, Paris 1946. In English: *Concerning Town Planning*, tr. by Clive Entwistle, Architectural Press, London 1947. — *U.N. Headquarters*, Reinhold, New York 1947. — *Plan de Buenos Ayres 1940*, propositions d'un plan directeur réalisable par étapes, Arquitectura de Hoy, Buenos Aires 1947. — *Le Modulor*, Essai sur une mesure harmonique à l'échelle humaine, applicable universellement à l'architecture et à la mécanique, Editions de l'Architecture d'Aujourd'hui, Boulogne-sur-Seine 1948. In English: *The Modulor*, tr. by Peter de Francia and Anna Bostock, Faber, London 1954. — *New World of Space*, Reynal and Hitchcock, New York, and The Institute of Contemporary Art, Boston 1948. — *Poésie sur Alger*, Falaize, Paris 1950. — *Une petite maison*, Girsberger, Zurich 1954. — *Modulor 2 - 1955 (La parole est aux usagers)*, suite de *Le Modulor, 1948*, Editions de l'Architecture d'Aujourd'hui, Boulogne-sur-Seine 1955. In English: *Modulor 2*, tr. by Peter de Francia and Anna Bostock, Faber, London 1958. — *Le Poème de l'angle droit*, with 19 color lithographs and many drawings, Verve, Paris 1955. — *Von der Poesie des Bauens*, Verlag Die Arche, Zurich 1957. — *Le poème électronique*, Editions de Minuit, Paris 1958. — *L'urbanisme des trois établissements humains*, Editions de Minuit, Paris 1959. — *L'Atelier de la recherche patiente*, preface by Maurice Jardot, Verlag Gerd Hatje, Stuttgart 1960. In English, tr. by James C. Palmes: *My Work*, Architectural Press, London 1960 and *Creation is a Patient Search*, Frederick A. Praeger, New York 1960. — *Mise au point*, Forces Vives, Paris 1966.

Complete Works

L. C. and Pierre Jeanneret, *Œuvre complète*, edited by Jean Badovici, 1st series, 1927; 2nd series, 1929; 3rd series, 1930; 4th series, 1931; 5th series, 1932; 6th series, 1933; 7th series, 1937, Editions Albert Morancé, Paris. — L. C. and Pierre Jeanneret, *Œuvre complète 1910-1929*, edited by W. Boesiger and O. Stonorov, Editions d'Architecture, Erlenbach

1929. — L. C. and Pierre Jeanneret, *Œuvre complète 1929-1934*, edited by W. Boesiger, Editions d'Architecture, Erlenbach 1935. — L. C. and Pierre Jeanneret, *Œuvre complète 1934-1938*, edited by Max Bill, Editions d'Architecture, Erlenbach 1939. — L. C., *Œuvre complète 1938-1946*, edited by W. Boesiger, Editions d'Architecture, Erlenbach 1946. — L. C., *Œuvre complète 1946-1952*, edited by W. Boesiger, Editions Girsberger, Zurich 1953. — L. C. and his atelier rue de Sèvres 35, *Œuvre complète 1952-1957*, edited by W. Boesiger, Editions Girsberger, Zurich 1958. — L. C. and his atelier rue de Sèvres 35, *Œuvre complète 1957-1965*, edited by W. Boesiger, Editions Girsberger, Zurich 1965. — *L. C. 1910-1960*, edited by Boesiger and Girsberger, Editions Girsberger, Zurich 1960. — *L. C. 1910-1965*, edited by Boesiger and Girsberger, Editions Girsberger, Zurich 1967.

Plastic Work

L. C., *Œuvre plastique, Peintures et Dessins, Architecture*, Editions Albert Morancé, Paris 1938. — Maurice Jardot, *L. C., Dessins*, Editions des Deux-Mondes, Paris 1955. — *L. C., Œuvre lithographique*, presented by E. Waeber, Bodmer, Zurich 1967. — *L. C., Dessins*, Forces vives, Paris 1968.

Monographs

Buildings and Projects

Alfred Roth, *Zwei Wohnhäuser von L. C. und Pierre Jeanneret*, preceded by *Fünf Punkte zu einer neuen Architektur*, von *L. C. und Pierre Jeanneret*, preface by Hans Hildebrandt, Akademischer Verlag Dr. F. Wedekind und Co., Stuttgart 1928. — *L'Ilot insalubre Nº 6*, Imprimerie André Tournon & Cie, Paris, May 1938. — L. C., *Les constructions « Murondins », Entreprise des jeunes, Gestion par les jeunes, Vitalisation des villages, Manuel technique publié sous le patronage du Secrétariat à la Jeunesse*, Etienne Chiron, Paris and Clermont-Ferrand 1942.

Apartment Blocks:

Unité d'Habitation à Marseille, Paris 1947 (special issue of *L'Homme et l'Architecture*, No. 11-14). — L. C., *L'Unité d'Habitation de Marseille*, Souillac-Mulhouse 1950 (special issue of *Le Point*, XXXVIII). In English: *The Marseilles Block*, tr. by Geoffrey Sainsbury, Harvill Press, London 1953. — *L. Cs. Wohneinheit Typ Berlin*, edited by Frithjof Müller-Rappen, Verlag für Fachliteratur, Berlin-Grunewald 1958. — P. Chombart de Lauwe and others, *Famille et Habitation, I. Sciences humaines et conceptions de l'habitation*, C.N.R.S., Paris 1959.

Ronchamp

Les chapelles du Rosaire à Vence, par Henri Matisse, et Notre-Dame-du-Haut à Ronchamp, par L. C., Editions du Cerf, Paris 1955. — Ernesto N. ROGERS, *La chapelle N.D. du Haut à Ronchamp de L. C.*, Editoriale Domus, Milan 1955-1956. — Anton HENZE, *Ronchamp, L. C.'s erster Kirchenbau*, Paulus Verlag, Recklinghausen 1956. — L. C., *Ronchamp*, Girsberger, Zurich and Hatje, Stuttgart 1957. In English: *The Chapel at Ronchamp*, tr. by Jacqueline Cullen, Architectural Press, London 1957. — Christoph W. DAVID, *Moderne Kirchen: Henri Matisse - Vence, Fernand Léger - Audincourt... L. C. - Ronchamp*, Die Arche, Zurich 1957. — Karl Anton Prinz ROHAN, *Besuch in Ronchamp*, Glock und Lutz, Nuremberg 1958. — L. C., *Le livre de Ronchamp*, Forces Vives, Paris 1961. — Dr MAULINI, *Comprendre Ronchamp*, Ronchamp 1964. — L. C., *Textes et dessins pour Ronchamp*, Forces Vives, Paris 1965. — R. BOLLE-REDDAT, *Wallfahrtskirche U.L. Frau auf der Höhe (N.D. du Haut), Ronchamp*, Schnell und Steiner, Munich and Zurich 1965. — *Journal de Notre-Dame-du-Haut*, quarterly edited by R. Bolle-Reddat, Chaplain of Ronchamp, since 1966.

La Tourette:

L. C., *Un couvent dominicain*, Editions du Cerf, Paris 1960 (special issue of the magazine *L'Art Sacré*). — *Le couvent Sainte-Marie-de-la-Tourette, construit par L. C.*, Editions du Cerf, Paris 1960. — Jean PETIT, *Un couvent de L. C.*, Forces Vives, Paris 1961. — Anton HENZE and Bernhard MOOS-BRUGGER, *La Tourette, L. Cs. Erster Klosterbau*, Verlag Keller, Starnberg 1963. In English: *L. C. - La Tourette*, Office du Livre Fribourg (Switzerland) 1966.

Chandigarh:

Norma EVENSON, *Chandigarh*, University of California Press, Berkeley and Los Angeles 1966.

Firminy:

Nello Smith, Jr., and R. Tansal (editors), *The Development by L. C. of the Design for "L'église de Firminy", a Church in France*, University of North Carolina Press, Raleigh 1964.

General Studies of Le Corbusier

François DE PIERREFEU, *L. C. et Pierre Jeanneret*, Crès, Paris 1930. — Maximilien GAUTHIER, *L. C., ou l'architecture au service de l'homme*, Denoel, Paris 1944. — Giancarlo De Carlo (editor), *L. C.*, Rosa & Ballo, Milan 1945. — BÉZARD, J. COUMMELIN-CONDOUIN, J. DAYRE, Hyacinthe DUBREUIL, L. C., LEYRITZ, HANNING, AUJAME, DE LOOZE, *Les Trois Etablissements humains*, Denoel, Paris 1946. — Stamo Papadaki (editor), *L. C., Architect, Painter, Writer*, essays by Joseph HUDNUT, Sigfried GIEDION, Fernand LÉGER, José Luis SERT, James THRALL SOBY, Macmillan, New York 1948. — Jean ALAZARD, *L. C.*, Electa, Milan and Hatier, Paris 1950. — W. S. VAN DE ERVE, *L. C., Idealistisch Architekt*, A. Oosthoeck, Utrecht 1951. — *Architecture du bonheur*, *L. C.*, texts by L. C. (*L'urbanisme est une clef*), Gabriel CHEREAU, Eugène Claudius PETIT, R. P. COUTURIER, Jean PETIT, André WOGENSCKY, Iannis XENAKIS, Presses de l'Ile de France, Paris 1955. — P. M. BARDI, *Lectura critica de/A Critical Review of L. C.*, Museu de Arte, Sao Paulo, n.d. (1955). — Anton HENZE, *L. C.*, Colloquium Verlag, Berlin-Dahlem 1957. — Henri PERRUCHOT, *L. C.*, Editions Universitaires, Paris 1958. — Françoise CHOAY, *L. C.*, George Braziller, New York 1960. — Jules ALAZARD and Jean-Pierre HÉBERT, *De la fenêtre au pan de verre dans l'œuvre de L. C.*, Glaces de Boussois, Paris 1961. — Peter BLAKE, *L. C., Architecture and Form*, Penguin Books, Baltimore and Harmondsworth 1964 (originally published in *The Master Builders*, Knopf, New York 1963). — Robert L. DELEVOY, *L. C.*, Paris 1963 (*Tendances*, No. 25, October 1963). — Sophie DARIA, *L. C., sociologue de l'urbanisme*, Seghers, Paris 1964. — Francesco TENTORI, *L. C.*, Compagnia Edizioni Internazionali, Milan 1965. — Saverio BUSIRI VICI, *Attualità di L. C.*, La Pace, Rome 1966. — Vittorio FRANCHETTI PARDO, *L. C.*, Sadea/Sansoni, Florence 1966 and Flammarion, Paris 1967. — Jean PETIT, *Le C. parle*, Forces Vives, Paris 1967. — Jacques RIBOUD, *Les erreurs de L. C. et leurs conséquences*, Editions Mazarines, Paris 1968. — Maurice BESSET, *L. C.* (in preparation).

Special Numbers of Magazines

L'Architecture d'Aujourd'hui, 1934, 1948. — *Casabella*, April 1963 (No. 274). — *Aujourd'hui*, November 1965 — *Architectural Forum*, October 1965. — *La Torre*, University of Porto Rico, January-April 1966.

Principal Retrospective Exhibitions

Catalogues, some of them very well documented, were issued for all these exhibitions.

1938, Zurich, Kunsthaus. — 1945, Minneapolis, Walker Art Center. — 1953, Paris, Musée d'Art Moderne (plastic work). — 1954, Bern, Kunsthalle. — 1957, Zurich, Kunsthaus (traveling exhibition shown all over the world). — 1962, Paris, Musée d'Art Moderne. — 1963, Florence, Palazzo Strozzi. — 1966, Prague, Vincenc Kramar Gallery. — 1966, Bratislava, Slovak National Gallery. — 1966, Paris, Musée des Arts Décoratifs. —

1966, Traveling exhibition organized by the students of the Ecole des Beaux-Arts, Nantes. — 1967, Oslo, National School of Architecture. — 1967, Stockholm. — 1968, Grenoble (audio-visual exhibition, catalogue-record).

General Works dealing at length with Le Corbusier

Walter GROPIUS, *Internationale Architektur*, Munich 1925. — Adolf BEHNE, *Der moderne Zweckbau*, Munich 1926. — G. A. PLATZ, *Die Baukunst der neuesten Zeit*, Berlin 1927. — H. R. HITCHCOCK and Philip JOHNSON, *International Style: Architecture Since 1922*, New York 1932. — Emil KAUFMANN, *Von Ledoux bis L. C.*, Vienna 1933. — Marie DORMOY, *L'Architecture française*, Paris 1938. — J. M. RICHARDS, *An Introduction to Modern Architecture*, Harmondsworth 1940. — Sigfried GIEDION, *Space, Time and Architecture*, Cambridge, Mass. 1941. — Alberto SARTORIS, *Introduzione all'architettura moderna*, Milan 1949. — Bruno ZEVI, *Storia dell'architettura moderna*, Turin 1950. — Arnold WHITTICK, *European Architecture in the 20th Century*, London 1950-1953. — Gillo DORFLES, *Barocco nell'architettura moderna*, Milan 1951. — Charalambos A. SFAELLOS, *Le fonctionnalisme dans l'architecture contemporaine*, Paris 1952. — P. A. MICHELIS, *L'esthétique de la construction de béton armé*, Athens n.d. — Sigfried GIEDION, *Architektur und Gemeinschaft*, Reinbek 1956. — Pierre FRANCASTEL, *Art et Technique aux XIXe et XXe siècles*, Paris 1956. — H. R. HITCHCOCK, *Architecture: Nineteenth and Twentieth Centuries*, Harmondsworth 1958. — Richard BIEDRZYNSKI,

Kirchen unserer Zeit, Munich 1958. — Jürgen JOEDICKE, *Geschichte der modernen Architektur*, Stuttgart 1958. — Reyner BANHAM, *Theory and Design in the First Machine Age*, London 1960. — Joseph PICHARD, *Eglises modernes à travers le monde*, Paris 1960. — Leonardo BENEVOLO, *Storia dell'architettura moderna*, Bari 1960. — G. E. KIDDER SMITH, *New Architecture in Europe*, New York 1961. — Vincent D. SCULLY Jr., *Modern Architecture*, New York 1962. — Reyner BANHAM, *A Guide to Modern Architecture*, London 1962. — Peter HAMMOND, *Toward a Church Architecture*, London 1962. — Lewis MUMFORD, *The Highway and the City*, New York 1963. — Gerd HATJE (editor), *Encyclopaedia of Modern Architecture*, London 1963. — G. E. KIDDER SMITH, *New Churches of Europe*, New York and London 1964. — Françoise CHOAY, *L'urbanisme: utopie et réalités*, Paris 1965. — Giorgio PICCINATO, *L'architettura contemporanea in Francia*, Bologna 1965. — Robert L. DELEVOY, *Dimensions du XXe siècle*, Geneva 1965. In English: *Dimensions of the 20th Century*, tr. by Stuart Gilbert, Geneva 1965. — John JACOBUS, *Die Architektur unserer Zeit. Zwischen Revolution und Tradition*, Stuttgart 1966. — Pietro SCURATI MANZONI, *Il Razionalismo. L'architettura dall'illuminismo alla reazione neo-espressionista*, Milan 1966. — Maurice BESSET, *Nouvelle Architecture Française/New French Architecture*, Teufen (Aarau, Switzerland) 1967 (English translation by James C. Palmes). — Amédée OZENFANT, *Mémoires*, Paris 1968. — J. JOEDICKE, J. and Chr. PLATH, *Die Weissenhofsiedlung*, Stuttgart 1968. — Georges MERCIER, *L'architecture religieuse contemporaine en France*, Tours 1968.

INDEX OF NAMES AND PLACES

LIST OF ILLUSTRATIONS

PUBLISHED OCTOBER 1968

TEXT AND ILLUSTRATIONS PRINTED IN OFFSET
BY IMPRIMERIES RÉUNIES S.A., LAUSANNE
UNDER THE TECHNICAL DIRECTION OF
EDITIONS D'ART ALBERT SKIRA, GENEVA

PHOTOGRAPHS

Unless otherwise specified in the List of Illustrations, all the photographs in this book were obligingly placed at our disposal by the Le Corbusier Foundation, Paris, or made at the Foundation on our behalf by Maurice Babey, Basel.

Printed in Switzerland